Designing and Improving Courses and Curricula in Higher Education

A Systematic Approach

Robert M. Diamond

Designing and Improving Courses and Curricula in Higher Education

A Systematic Approach

Jossey-Bass Publishers · San Francisco

DESIGNING AND IMPROVING COURSES AND CURRICULA IN HIGHER EDUCATION
A Systematic Approach
by Robert M. Diamond

Copyright © 1989 by: Jossey-Bass Inc., Publishers
350 Sansome Street
San Francisco, California 94104

Library of Congress Cataloging-in-Publication Data

Diamond, Robert M.
  Designing and improving courses and curricula in
higher education.

  (The Jossey-Bass higher education series)
  Bibliography: p.
  Includes index.
    1. Universities and colleges — United States —
Curricula — Evaluation.   2. Curriculum planning — United
States   I. Title.   II. Series
LB2361.5.D5   1989   378'.199'0973   88-28433
ISBN 1-55542-129-6

Manufactured in the United States of America

The paper used in this book is acid-free and meets the
State of California requirements for recycled paper
(50 percent recycled waste, including 10 percent
postconsumer waste), which are the strictest guidelines
for recycled paper currently in use in the United States.

Credits are on page 279.

JACKET DESIGN BY WILLI BAUM

FIRST EDITION
HB Printing   10 9 8 7 6 5 4

Code 8902

The Jossey-Bass
Higher Education Series

Contents

ix

Tables, Figures, and Exhibits

Chapter Five

Chapter Six

Chapter Seven

Chapter Eight

Chapter Ten

Chapter Eleven

Preface

Higher education in the United States is undergoing unprecedented public scrutiny. National studies sponsored by such agencies as the National Endowment for the Humanities, the National Institute of Education (NIE), the Association of American Colleges (AAC), and The Carnegie Foundation for the Advancement of Teaching have all identified significant systemic problems. Their findings point to a need to create orderly, effective change in curricula, set new priorities for faculty, and establish systems for evaluating and rewarding success in teaching.

Of these three topics, the one with which this volume is concerned is the need to reexamine curricula and make appropriate changes. The AAC findings (Association of American Colleges, 1985) identified essential content and skills for which the evaluators felt higher education programs should assume responsibility:

1. Inquiry: abstract and logical thinking and critical analysis
2. Literacy: writing, reading, speaking, and listening
3. An understanding of numerical data
4. Historical consciousness

5. An ability to distinguish science from other kinds of inquiry
6. A sense of values: the ability to make choices and to accept responsibility for them
7. Appreciation of and experiences in the arts
8. International and multicultural experience

Similarly, Ernest Boyer's preface to the Carnegie report *College: The Undergraduate Experience in America* (The Carnegie Foundation for the Advancement of Teaching, 1986) calls for an "integrated core curriculum" leading from "essential knowledge" through interdisciplinary connections that facilitate "developments and integrate community service, political participation, [and] application of knowledge to life beyond the campus." Boyer also cited the need for institutions to make clear mission statements and to reflect in their programs the value they place on teaching and research. He recommended orientation programs that introduce entering students to the values and traditions of higher education and courses that provide a strong, integrated core, including attention to the communication skills cited in the AAC report previously mentioned.

The National Endowment for the Humanities report *To Reclaim a Legacy* (Bennett, 1984) echoes the call for an undergraduate curriculum that provides a strong core of knowledge of the humanities and values teaching, and is characterized by cooperation between administrators and faculty in moving toward constructive change in their programs. Although the twenty-seven specific recommendations of the NIE report *Involvement in Learning: Realizing the Potential of American Higher Education* (National Institute of Education, 1984) focus on similar categories of change, they emphasize the need to show demonstrable improvement in effects on students' knowledge, capacities, skills, and attitudes between entrance and graduation. The NIE report stresses further that these demonstrable improvements should occur within established, clearly expressed, and publicly announced standards of performance, and it directs the colleges toward efficient, cost-effective use of student and institutional resources of time, effort, and money.

These reports present a clear call for imaginative plan-

ning in which faculty, administrators, and students work together toward change. They look toward curricula that take
advantage of technological developments and integrate community service, political participation, and other opportunities for
civic responsibility into the curriculum. Although they call for
significant change in content and pedagogy, they do not describe how these changes might be made.

Often institutions, departments, or instructors recognize
significant problems in the content and design of curricula or
courses, but their efforts to change are hampered by uncertainty
about how to make orderly changes. They are uncertain about
where to begin and what roles faculty, curriculum committees,
and administrators should play. They need help in isolating the
questions that need to be addressed and finding the sources of
information that will enable them to reach their goals.

*Designing and Improving Courses and Curricula in Higher
Education* responds to the needs of institutions, departments,
and faculty who recognize a need for change but are unsure of
how to effectively reach their goals as well as to the needs of those
who may be directly involved as change agents. The chapters
focus on an approach that has been used at institutions with
very different profiles: private and public, large and small, and
with varying budgets. It offers an in-depth, longitudinal study of
one approach to systemic change. The book shows how to move
from concept to actualization, from theory to practice. Case
studies illustrate the adaptability of the model to broad curricular change and to course and program design, where it operates
with equal success.

Several factors make this model particularly relevant. Programs that have been developed using the model meet the goals
identified in recent major reports on educational change. Faculty who have used the model have a real sense of ownership of
the projects and programs developed, ensuring that these outcomes will become part of the existing system and thus survive.
Compared with other approaches, the approach recommended
here is cost effective and provides visible results in the shortest
possible time.

In the decade or so since the model's first use, changes

incorporated as a result of experience in working with it and comments from faculty and staff have simplified the model and made it easier to use. These changes have reduced the time needed for implementation. Program assessment is a part of the process and places the importance of outcome measurement of the course and curriculum within the context of national, state, and regional goals.

The approach described in this book has several additional characteristics that significantly affect its success. Although these are thoroughly discussed in succeeding chapters, a word about them here is appropriate. By using a noncontent expert to facilitate the design process, this model allows the faculty to focus on content and structure while ensuring that assumptions are questioned and alternatives explored. The model also allows faculty to focus first on what an ideal program would look like, eliminating perceived limitations—many of which turn out to be more imagined than real. Furthermore, it is data driven, using information from a wide range of sources to help determine scope, content, effectiveness, and efficiency. This systems model places technology in perspective, using it where and when it is appropriate. Finally, and equally important, although this approach requires hard work, faculty find it exciting, challenging, and rewarding, and administrators remark on its efficiency and effectiveness.

Purposes and Audiences

Many books have been written about teaching and learning. But that is not the focus of this book. It is a practical, descriptive handbook with several major purposes and audiences:

- It is a guide for *administrators* on how to develop and support a climate and a program aimed at improving instruction.
- It provides *faculty* with one effective model for designing, implementing, and evaluating courses and curricula.
- It suggests design options that are available to *those involved*

in the design process as efforts are made to meet the diverse needs of their students.

• It provides *staff members of instructional or faculty development offices* with guidelines and techniques that can improve their effectiveness and increase their impact.

This book, while based on sound theory, is not a theoretical discourse. It focuses on how to approach and implement the redesigning of the structure within which teaching takes place — the courses and the curricula. It is a practical guide for faculty and administrators interested in improving the quality and effectiveness of their academic programs.

The suggestions are derived from my own experience and the experience of my associates in various institutions in which I have worked in the field of instructional development. Most case studies are drawn from the records of Syracuse University's Center for Instructional Development. *Designing and Improving Courses and Curricula in Higher Education* is designed to share with others the strategies that have worked well in making constructive, considered change of the sort higher education is presently challenged to initiate.

Overview of the Contents

The book covers five major areas.

1. *The model: an overview (Chapter One):* This chapter reviews the characteristics and strengths of the model we are using and discusses the reasons for its selection.

2. *Implementing the model (Chapters Two through Ten):* These highly practical chapters, which represent the major portion of the book, examine the model using case studies from such varied disciplines as English, mathematics, and religion. These case studies, ranging from single courses (graduate and undergraduate) to entire curricula, include comments from participating faculty. They are presented in a step-by-step manner that identifies the specific questions that were asked, the alternatives that were explored, and

the reasons for the choices that were made. In addition, the specific case studies have been selected to provide the reader with a wide range of replicable applications. The chapters in this section follow the model and move from project generation and selection (Chapter Two) to a description of the initial design meeting (Chapter Three) to a discussion of the types of information that are needed to make design decisions (Chapter Four) and a discussion of the realm and process of thinking in the ideal (Chapter Five) to the practical considerations of implementation; the stating of objectives and measurement of student performance; design and material production; the preparation of a manual for students; and implementation, evaluation, and revision of new curricula (Chapters Six through Ten).

3. *Establishing an instructional support agency (Chapter Eleven):* Written primarily for administrators, this chapter describes the organization, location, budget, and staff of an administrative unit charged with the support of course and curriculum design on a campuswide basis. A number of practical recommendations on such topics as faculty released time versus summer employment, copyright and royalty policies, and so forth are included.

4. *Lessons learned (Chapter Twelve):* This brief but very important chapter highlights many of the important lessons that have been learned about course and curriculum design and evaluation.

5. *Resources:* The final portion of the book includes a number of useful evaluation protocols, sample forms, and materials.

Acknowledgments

I would like to express my appreciation to Donald Ely and Philip Doughty for their insight and for their encouragement to complete the manuscript; to Bette Gaines for her editing assistance; to Peter Gray, who is responsible for many of the evaluation instruments found in these pages; to Martha Strain for her graphics; to June Mermigos and Allison Brown for their work on the many flowcharts in this book; to "Dame" Elinor

Wilson and Nancy Sweeney, who somehow survived the writing, editing, and revision process; and most of all to the staff of the Center for Instructional Development and the faculty at Syracuse University, who participated in the design, implementation, and evaluation of the many courses, curricula, and programs described in this book.

Manlius, New York   Robert M. Diamond
November 1988

To the many talented individuals—faculty, administrators, and support staff—who have committed themselves to improving the quality of higher education
and to Dolores Diamond for her encouragement, humor, and capacity for putting up with just about everything

The Author

Robert M. Diamond is assistant vice-chancellor for instructional development, director of the Center for Instructional Development, and professor of education at Syracuse University. He received his B.A. degree (1951) in economics from Union College and his M.A. degree (1953) in health education and Ph.D. degree (1962) in educational communications from New York University, where he received the Founders Day Award for Outstanding Scholarship.

Diamond's major professional focus has been on the systematic improvement of instruction in higher education. He has directed course and curriculum design, implementation, and evaluation programs and activities at San Jose State University; the University of Miami; the State University of New York, Fredonia; and Syracuse University. A Senior Fulbright Lecturer to India in 1976, he was selected as a distinguished faculty member for the State University of New York Scholar Exchange Program in 1969. Diamond is editor of *A Guide to Evaluating Teaching for Promotion and Tenure* (1987) and author or coauthor of several other books, including *A Guide to Instructional Television* (1964), *The Amateur Psychologist's Dictionary* (1966), and *Instructional Development for Individual Learning in Higher Education* (1974). He also wrote the sections on instructional design in the *International*

Encyclopaedia of Education (1986) and the *International Encyclopaedia of Technology* (1988).

Diamond has served as a consultant to numerous colleges and universities in the United States and abroad and is past president of the Division of Instructional Development, Association of Educational Communication and Technology.

1

Benefits of
a Systematic Approach
to Course and
Curriculum Improvement

After we discuss the need for a sequential approach to
course and curriculum improvement, the model we will use is
introduced and the roles of participants are defined.

Overview

National studies may call for change; states and national
accrediting agencies may require institutions to redefine their
goals and to determine whether or not they achieve them; and
students, faculty, and staff may proclaim that improvements are
needed; however, what happens in the classroom will, in the long
run, determine whether these improvements take place. Ernest
Boyer, in his book *College, the Undergraduate Experience in America*
(1987), points out that the changes that are necessary are not
inconsequential. "The undergraduate college, the very heart of
higher learning, is a troubled institution. In a society that makes
different and contrary demands upon higher education, many
of the nation's colleges are more successful in credentialing than
in providing a quality education for their students. . . . We
found divisions on the campus, conflicting priorities and com-
peting interests that diminish the intellectual and social quality

of the undergraduate experience and restrict the capacity of the college effectively to serve its students" (p. 2).

Traditionally, course improvement has been the responsibility of the faculty member, and efforts to redesign curricula are usually assigned to departmental committees established specifically for this purpose. In many instances, the faculty involved have devoted significant time and energy to these activities despite the fact that often they received little recognition for their efforts, no matter how successful these projects were. Some of these activities have resulted in exciting new courses, revised curricula, such innovations in teaching as self-paced science laboratories, new courses in science for the nonscience major, and numerous applications of computer-assisted instruction, which have been both effective and exciting. Other projects that have received little departmental, administrative, or collegial support have not been as successful.

Since we are working with limited resources (faculty, time, and money), it is imperative that we use them well. The process that we use must be effective, efficient, and politically sensitive. All too often excellent new experimental programs have been unable to acquire the necessary departmental or institutional approvals or have failed to survive after the excitement of innovation has passed. Thus, we must concern ourselves not only with the design of new or improved programs but with their implementation as well. Experiences on a number of campuses have shown that for significant academic improvements to occur and be retained several conditions are essential.

- The faculty must have ownership in the process, retaining responsibility for teaching and academic content.
- The academic administration of the institution must support these activities and provide the resources necessary for these efforts to be successful.
- Priorities must be established, projects selected, and resources allocated accordingly.
- Evaluation must be an integral part of the process, with the success of all instructionally related projects being measured on the basis of changes in student performance.

- A support team must be available for planning, production, implementation, and institutionalization.
- The procedures that are followed not only must address each of the above issues but must be systematically designed to provide maximum impact for the investment of time and money.

In addition, faculty and administration must cooperate to ensure that a reward system that encourages teaching and learning exists. The need for such change is particularly significant at research institutions, where teaching and research must be equally valued if improvements in the academic programs are to occur. In too many instances those faculty working on projects related to teaching do so knowing that these activities reduce the time they can spend on research or writing and may actually diminish their chances for promotion, tenure, or significant salary increases.

While we will be focusing on courses and curriculum, we should also keep in mind that what goes on in the classroom cannot be separated from the total instructional experience of students. No matter how effective we are as teachers, and no matter how well-designed our courses and curricula are, we will not be successful if our libraries are not conducive to studying, if our residence halls provide our students with little personal support, if few opportunities for recreation exist, and if we, as faculty, are rarely available to meet with students outside of the classroom, laboratory, or studio. Optimum learning requires a rich social, cultural, and physical environment. Such a setting does not happen by chance; it must be nurtured and planned and must involve the participation of staff from the offices of student affairs, residential life, and numerous other offices throughout the institution.

Need for an Effective Approach

The needs for instructional improvement are too great and resources are too limited to allow us to be inefficient or ineffective in the way we address our problems. We cannot afford to leave things to chance, hoping that the right question will be asked, the key people will be involved, and all the appropriate options will be explored. For this reason we turn to a model for course and curriculum design that provides the faculty with the "ownership" they need and the administration with guidelines leading toward maximum impact on the institution.

Why a Model? Following a specific, effective model for course or curriculum design provides those who are involved in the project with several important advantages.

- It identifies the key factors that should be considered in a sequential order.
- It serves as a procedural guide for those directing the project.
- It allows those involved to understand where they are in the process and their role within it.
- It improves efficiency by reducing duplication of effort and ensuring that critical questions are asked and alternative solutions explored.

Common Characteristics. Hannun and Briggs (1980), in their analysis of instructional system designs, found seven common elements among them.

1. Planning, development, delivery, and evaluation of instruction were based on systems theory.
2. Goals were based on an analysis of the environment of the system. For example, a two-year college will, and must, have different goals from those of a university.
3. Instructional objectives were stated in terms of performance.
4. The design of the program was sensitive to the entering competencies of the students and of their short- and long-term academic goals.
5. Considerable attention was paid to planning instructional strategies and selecting media.
6. Evaluation was part of the design and revision process.
7. Students were measured and graded by their ability to

achieve desired standards and criteria rather than by comparing one student with another.

Models designed by Briggs (1970), Gerlach and Ely (1980), Kemp (1977), and Russell and Johanningsmeir (1981) are representative approaches that include these characteristics while focusing on course and lesson design.

Other models are more narrowly focused. Concerns about needs assessment explored by Kaufman and English (1979) and the work of Wittich and Schuller (1979) on the use of technology are examples of models that can be used within steps of models that focus on course, curriculum, or program design. Also included in this category would be models designed to assist in decision making in lesson design, such as Merrill (1977) on learning hierarchies, Keller (1978) on using motivation in teaching, and Popham and Baker (1970) on selecting instructional activities.

While these approaches are, for the most part, effective in doing what they claim to do, they have one or more of the following limitations.

- They tend not to question *what* is being taught but focus primarily on improving the delivery and effectiveness of instruction.
- They tend to be suitable for use in a single course rather than in curriculum projects or other efforts that are larger in scope.
- They tend to narrow, rather than broaden, the focus of those who use them.
- They rarely address the political concerns of project implementation and survival.

The process of designing, implementing, and evaluating a course or curriculum is complex. It requires (1) a sensitivity to the academic setting of the project, (2) an awareness of the capabilities, interests, and priorities of the students the program is designed to serve, (3) a knowledge and appreciation of the discipline, (4) an understanding of the resources and options available to the faculty involved, (5) an understanding of those instructional goals that are required of all students, regardless of their major and long-term personal goals. The approach that is used must contain these elements and, at the same time, be easy to understand and to use.

An Introduction to Our Model

The model we will use (Figure 1), first developed by the author at the University of Miami in the early 1960s, has undergone a number of significant revisions. However, after use with a broad range of courses and curricula and by a large number of faculty and support staff, it has, for the last ten years or so, remained structurally unchanged. Those using this model at a number of institutions report that it is easily understood, efficient, and effective. The model is less complicated than most models of its type and requires less time between start and implementation than others. The costs involved are also less. In addition, as will be noted through a number of examples, it can be used to design and implement courses, curricula, and other instructionally related projects.

The model has two basic phases: (1) project selection and design and (2) production, implementation, and evaluation. Like most models, it is generally sequential, requiring that certain steps be completed before others begin. Although this model, like most others, will appear to be linear in its overall design (Step 1 to Step 2 to Step 3, and so on), this appearance is somewhat deceptive. Ideally, some actions must precede others, and certain decisions should not be made until all relevant facts are known. However, in practice, all of the data may not be available when an initial decision is required; information collected later may contradict earlier data suggesting a different decision, or those involved may, for a number of reasons, wish to focus on an issue that is somewhat out of sequence. The model allows this flexibility. Experience has shown that, although the overall flow of the model is generally followed, the sequence is never as linear as it appears (see Figure 2).

In addition to the simplicity of its design, the model has

Figure 1. Process for Educational Program Development.

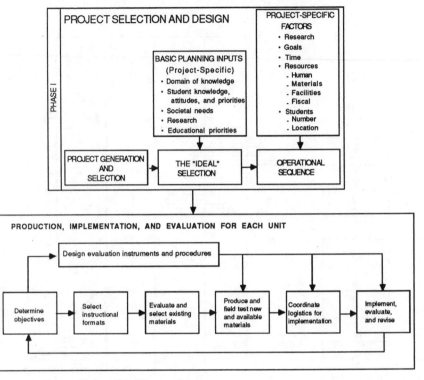

Source: Robert M. Diamond.

five major characteristics that, when combined, differentiate it from most others.

1. It forces those using it to think in ideal terms.
2. It encourages the use of diagrams to show structure and content.
3. It relies heavily on the use of data.
4. It encourages the team approach.
5. It is politically sensitive.

   Thinking in the Ideal. The initial goal of the design phase is to develop the "ideal" course or curriculum. When completed, the diagram that is developed represents the best possible in-

Figure 2. Work Flow by Time.

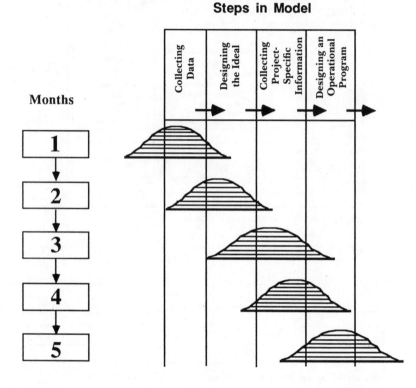

structional sequence for meeting the goals of the course or program. We have found it most efficient to start with the ideal and then modify it according to the specific administrative, material, and human constraints that exist. Limiting the original design to meet anticipated constraints tends to limit the creativity and openness of the process and thus results in an inferior product. Another reason for trying to develop an optimum design is that anticipated limitations or constraints are often more perceived than real: "How do you know you can't do something until you try?" The final design evolves slowly with many revisions as new data are provided and various viewpoints are discussed.

Even though working toward the ideal is an exciting part of the design process, it is not always easy. Many faculty find it extremely difficult to imagine abandoning the time frames, credit structures, course syllabi, and textbooks that they are accustomed to using. Comments from faculty who have been through the process of thinking in the ideal have been generally positive.

- It forced us to "stretch" for the ultimate rather than starting out settling only for those things that we thought were possible.
- I was initially resistant to the "ideal" approach because I tend to be a pragmatic person who works and plans on the basis of resources available. However, once I got past the "typical mentality," the freedom afforded by imaginative play in the ideal mode brought forth a number of surprising and positive ideas.
- Initially, the question was a challenge to abandon traditional assumptions about how the college classroom "should" look or work. That created the opportunity to consider faculty roles other than lecturer/demonstrator. I had great reservations about changing my role in the classroom. However, when I realized that, in the ideal, I could cover more materials in greater depth with adequate and better comprehension on the part of the students, I got very excited.
- There was no threat of failure in working with the ideal.
- Thinking in the ideal is an exciting and intellectually rewarding experience that allows the planners to test assumptions about content; about the students, their goals, abilities, and priorities; and about structure and methodology.

Use of Diagrams. Simple diagrams provide an excellent method of visualizing an entire course or curriculum and for showing relationships and sequence. For these reasons, these diagrams will be used in this book to help illustrate the actual process of course and curriculum design. These diagrams are examples of specific courses and curricula that have been developed using this model.

Boxes and arrows in such diagrams can sometimes be confusing when they are first used, but the technique of diagraming has, nevertheless, proven to be an extremely helpful communication device. A diagram showing the elements of a program in their proper sequence can (1) clarify the scope of the project; (2) help identify gaps, overlaps, and sequencing problems; (3) facilitate modifications; and, perhaps most important, (4) clarify communication between those working on a project, and later, when the program is offered, between faculty and students. Experience has shown that using such terms as "in any order," "as required," or "as selected" can substantially reduce the complexity of many flow charts. While at first not everyone is comfortable with this technique, faculty tend to change their thinking once its practicality becomes obvious.

- My first reaction was that all "those people" were addicted to rectangles and arrows, probably since the first grade. Over time, I appreciated the help of "visual" memory in rethinking and reconstructing course projects. It enables "time" to be visualized as well as relating subject matter and ideas to each other.
- I first thought it was too simplistic to capture the overlap built into a course, but with use I grew to see its merits rather than limitations.
- What a help; why didn't I think of it?

As stressed earlier, the earlier designs of a course or curriculum will represent the "ideal." Later versions will represent what actually was offered in the program. Specifically, the diagram will identify each of the major instructional components and the sequence in which they occur. During this stage the focus is on topics and elements of the program, not on how instruction will take place. An example of this type of preliminary outline is shown in Figure 3.

By the time the design phase is completed, the diagram will include (if appropriate to the specific course or curriculum)

- The step-by-step flow chart of the course content or, in the case of curriculum design, the overall sequence of courses

Figure 3. Preliminary Outline: International Relations.

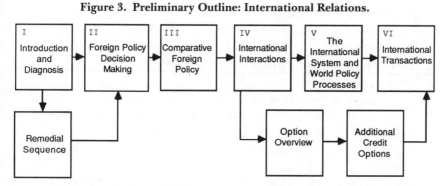

Source: William Coplin, Michael O'Leary, Paul Eickmann, Robert M. Diamond.

- When, in the total sequence, *orientation* and *diagnostic testing* sessions are scheduled
- What elements of the program are essential and are required of all students—that is, what is the instructional "core" (particularly important in curriculum projects)
- What specific *remedial units* must be available for the students and when they should be completed in relation to the other elements of the program
- Where *student options* are included and what topics should be considered in these options (It also may be possible at this time to identify which options may be available for additional credit.)
- Where *seminars, faculty conferences, large group sessions,* and *independent study assignments* are essential or recommended
- Where separate tracks for *specialization* exist
- Which instructional components have objectives that some students already have reached; that is, where exemptions can be anticipated based on the data on entering levels of competency
- Where, in the case of courses, evaluation will take place

The amount of detail shown in a particular component outline is directly related to how far along the design process is and to the scope of the program being developed: the farther along the project is, the more detailed the diagram will be. In a curriculum project, a diagram might be used to emphasize the interrelationship of major components and courses. In a single course the early diagram drafts would emphasize main elements and their basic sequence.

Each of the larger elements will in turn be broken down into a more detailed component outline. For example, Figure 4 (pp. 14–15) is a detailed description of one of the sections (Module 5, International Interactions) in Figure 3. (It should be noted that in the later version of the diagram the number of this unit has changed.) A single course will usually consist of four, five, or even more of these major module or unit outlines. Usually for convenience and clarity, each module will represent a somewhat self-contained unit of the course, covering several weeks of study, with its own set of objectives, options, and evaluation. In Figure 3, six such modules or segments of the course have been identified.

While these diagrams should be as specific as possible, they should not be considered final or static. The diagram, as will be noted in the sections that follow, may undergo constant and sometimes significant modifications as the preliminary (ideal) concepts are translated into operation and are field tested. However, the more specific and detailed the design, the clearer the goals and the easier and more rapid the transition will be from design into actual implementation.

Use of Data. As noted earlier, this model has two major phases: Phase I—project selection and design—and Phase II—production, implementation, and evaluation. Decision making in each of these steps relies heavily on the collection and use of data. Whether accurate data help clarify the problems that have been identified, provide information about the students or the professional field, or measure student performance, accurate data are essential if the course or curriculum developed is to be successful. As will be seen as different steps are discussed, data play a major role in both the design and implementation stages. In our model, data will be used to

- Confirm and clarify the problem that is being addressed
- Provide information essential to the design of the program

- Provide information during the field testing of the program that is essential for revision (data on learning, logistics, material effectiveness, and so on)
- Provide information for final evaluation of the program and for use in reporting the results of the project to external publics, such as funding agencies, administrators, and others interested in the project

The Team Approach. For a project to be successful, a number of talents are needed. Ideally this team will be composed of faculty, an instructional developer, an evaluator, and production people.

The key to any project is quality faculty — faculty who not only have the necessary experience and content expertise but also are willing to devote the time and energy that will be required. In curriculum projects it is essential that each major academic area be represented. In course projects the senior faculty responsible for that course or other experts may provide essential content expertise. The selection of the participants is often a major step in determining a project's success. In most cases several faculty should be involved to provide a broader content base and faculty backup in case one faculty member leaves, is assigned to other courses, or is promoted into an administrative position.

Surprising as it may seem at first, one of the most useful people on a project is someone with teaching or professional experience *outside* the content area involved. At some institutions, such as Syracuse University, an instructional developer is a trained professional who has experience in design, understands teaching and the use of technology, and, most importantly, can work well with faculty in a supportive role.

By coming to the project without the discipline's vocabulary and without the traditional viewpoints of the profession, this person can test assumptions and, without being a threat, question what is being done and why. For example, if the content or vocabulary of a project is unclear to this person, it may well be unclear to the students. In a sense, the developer is a surrogate student. In addition, the developer might suggest new options and raise questions the faculty may not have considered. On

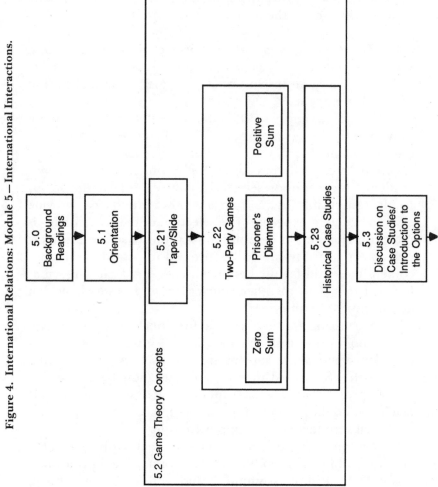

Figure 4. International Relations: Module 5 — International Interactions.

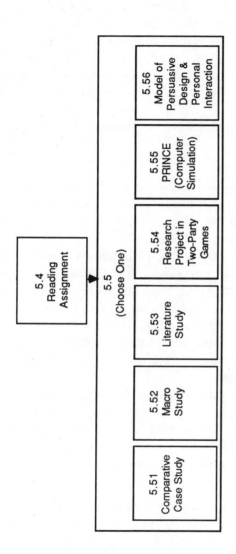

Note: After studying a series of background readings (5.0) designed to familiarize the students with international interactions, the students attend an orientation describing the content and design of the module (5.1). The first major instructional unit is an independent study sequence on game theory concepts (5.2). After viewing an introductory tape/slide sequence (5.21), pairs of students participate in several games (5.22) and then individually apply game concepts to historical case studies (5.23). Discussions growing out of the game situations follow (5.3). After a brief introduction to the six options, all students demonstrate their ability in a variety of ways, based upon which option they choose (5.5), to assess the relative merits of a bargaining strategy suggested by Roger Fisher in his book *International Conflicts for Beginners*. Students are also given some flexibility as to the manner in which they will report their findings (that is, written report, taped report, tape/slide report, or debate).

Source: William Coplin, Michael O'Leary, Paul Eickmann.

campuses where such a person does not exist, an experienced, successful, and innovative faculty member from another discipline should be asked to serve in this capacity. It should be noted that individuals who can serve effectively in this role are not always easy to find, for, not only do they need a range of human skills and a firm knowledge of education and teaching, but they also must be willing to work in a supportive role in a project that is not theirs but belongs to the faculty they are assisting. They are also people who are at home with new ideas and supportive of innovation.

It is interesting to view how this "outsider's" role has been perceived by faculty.

- Not being from the same discipline removed the professional competition. The questions were marvelously facilitative and clarifying. We became aware of our assumptions. Elegant. Simple.
- It was wonderful working with someone from another discipline, because this person could give me an objective opinion of my work. It helped me to clarify what I was teaching.
- It is hard for faculty to believe that someone who is not a subject matter specialist can be of help in assessing or promoting the criticism and construction of a course. However, with quality personnel, the "fresh" eye and "naive" questions often open new insights.
- Involving a person from outside my discipline prevented me from making assumptions. Kept me organized. The ability of this person to ask "dumb" questions constantly reminded me of a professorial tendency to assume students know things they do not—could not—possibly know.

The role of the developer is to chair working meetings, to bring to these meetings other resource people as appropriate, to ensure that the model is being followed, and, equally important, to make sure that the project team keeps moving. A basic and most useful bibliography for individuals interested in or assigned to serve in this role will be found at the end of this chapter. A further discussion of the roles of the developer and of the evaluator will be found in Chapter Eleven.

Unlike the instructional developer, the evaluator attends only those meetings that are essential to his or her job of data collecting, interpreting, and reporting. While some data can be collected by others on the team, there are occasions when specialized skills and objectivity are essential. Not only must the evaluator have a firm understanding of how different types of data can be collected, for these projects this person must also have the ability to write and communicate effectively to those outside of the field.

As required, projects will also need secretarial assistance and the services of specialists in graphics and media production. Individuals with these production skills are usually available through the audiovisual unit of most institutions.

Additional Characteristics. If there is one word that determines the life expectancy of a project, it is *ownership.* Many projects, often effective ones, die as the result of neglect or antagonism on the part of administrators, other faculty, or key academic committees. By involving these various groups from the very beginning in the project selection and design process, the model helps generate the political support and ownership that are required for implementation and approval. If faculty who feel they should be consulted are not, if administrators who will have to provide resources for implementation know little about the project, or if little attention is paid to the steps that must be followed for formal approval, there is little chance that the new program, no matter how good it is, will survive. Our model ensures that work does not begin until the proper faculty and administrators are involved and supportive and that a climate for success exists.

All too often faculty begin a course redesign with a mental set of what the program will look like, which media they will use, in effect picking the solution before they have defined the problem. In this model such decisions are delayed until all factors are considered and an effort is made to use that specific medium or combination of media that is most appropriate.

Summary

The systems model we will use in subsequent chapters is not a traditional one. More comprehensive than most, it forces faculty to think in the ideal and uses a noncontent developer to direct faculty through the process. Relying on flow diagrams to show content and structure, the model is both effective and efficient and is one with which faculty are comfortable. In the chapters that follow, we will use a number of case studies to illustrate the use of the model in courses and curricula that have been developed.

A Supplementary Bibliography for Developers

An instructional developer, or faculty member serving in the role of facilitator, must understand the consultative role and have at his or her disposal a number of specific competencies and techniques. The references included in this bibliography serve as an excellent information base for individuals moving into this complex and crucial role. The list was compiled by Barbara M. Florini, formerly associate director of development at Syracuse University's Center for Instructional Development.

Organization and Management

Cook, D. L. *Educational Project Management.* Westerville, Ohio: Merrill, 1971.

Hersey, P., and Blanchard, K. H. *Management of Organizational Behavior: Utilizing Human Resources.* (3rd ed.) Englewood Cliffs, N.J.: Prentice-Hall, 1977.

Schein, E. H. *Process Consultation: Its Role in Organization Development.* Reading, Mass.: Addison-Wesley, 1969.

Zaltman, G., and Duncan, R. *Strategies for Planned Change.* New York: Wiley, 1977.

Zaltman, G., and others. *Dynamic Educational Change.* New York: Free Press, 1977.

Skills and Techniques

Benjamin, A. *The Helping Interview.* (2nd ed.) Boston: Houghton Mifflin, 1974. (An introduction to effective questioning techniques.)

Bertcher, H. J. *Group Participation: Techniques for Leaders and Members.* Beverly Hills, Calif.: Sage, 1979.

Hanks, K., and others. *Design Yourself.* Los Altos, Calif.: William Kaufmann, 1978. (Suggestions for creative problem solving.)

Hon, D. *Meetings That Matter: A Self-Teaching Guide.* New York: Wiley, 1980.

Koberg, D. *Universal Traveler.* Los Altos, Calif.: William Kaufmann, 1976.

Payne, S. L. *Art of Asking Questions.* Princeton, N.J.: Princeton University Press, 1980.

2

Making the Decision to Create or Redesign a Course or Program

This chapter focuses on two essential steps that must be completed before a project begins: generating potential projects and selecting those that should be undertaken. Different approaches for generating projects are discussed, and a procedure for selecting projects is described.

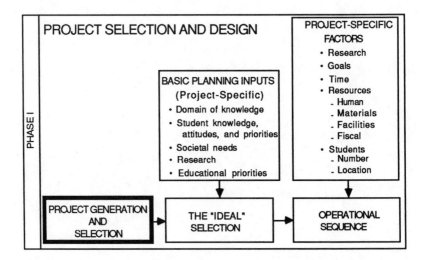

Overview

A decision to create or redesign a course or curriculum should not be taken lightly, since it will require committing a great deal of time and effort. In addition, entering into this activity can have a direct impact on the professional careers of the faculty involved. For some, particularly nontenured individuals at research universities, there may even be an element of risk. Before a project is begun, a number of factors must be considered: (1) how important the project is to the academic department, school, or college, and, when appropriate, even to the institution, (2) how the project will be received by others, (3) whether the necessary support is available, and (4) if the required faculty commitment will be made.

While most models for course and curriculum design identify a formal needs assessment as their first step, this is not where projects actually begin. A systematic needs assessment occurs only after some person or group has concluded that a problem exists. A formal needs assessment does two things. It defines the problem in specific terms and generates specific information that will be needed in the design phase of the project. Before such a formal needs assessment is mounted, however, be sure that those involved are committed to beginning the project and that the support necessary for success exists. Without this commitment and a real potential for success, engaging in a course or curriculum development project not only is a waste of time and money but can create a great deal of frustration and anxiety as significant problems are identified, and then nothing is done to correct them.

Why Projects Begin

Faculty become involved with course or curriculum projects for a variety of reasons. For example, they may be convinced that the content of the course is outdated, or they may be concerned with a high failure or dropout rate; graduates may be telling them, informally, that when they left the institution, they were not prepared for their career choices. In some instances, faculty may have become increasingly concerned with their students' attitudes, a diminishing number of majors entering the field, or a perceived lowering in the quality of their students. Some faculty may have simply become bored with what they were doing—the "academic seven-year itch." Some course or curricular projects begin when those teaching in the program find that they are no longer covering all they wish to and conclude that changes must be made. Other projects are undertaken as a direct reaction to concerns expressed by employers, the fiscal need for larger enrollments, or a strong desire on the part of an entire department to update or improve program quality. Some projects begin when a faculty member becomes intrigued with a new instructional approach or technology and finds that to use it well, he or she must first address some basic questions that have been avoided for years.

Questions to Consider

Whether the identification of a problem is based on hard data, hunches, vague feelings of frustration, or the desire to engage in a challenging and perhaps even enjoyable exercise, several questions should be asked before work begins. These questions constitute the evaluation component at the project selection step of the design phase. Most often at this time, these informal evaluation activities are performed by those most directly involved in making the decision on whether or not to begin a project.

How Important Is the Project to the Department, to Faculty, and to the Chairperson and/or Dean? If there is little support for what is proposed, if few see the need or perceive the stated problem, if there are other problems that they feel are more important to deal with, beginning the project may be a major mistake. There will be not only little support or assistance for the effort but significant difficulty in getting needed approval from key committees and administrative offices.

If key faculty are coming up for tenure in the next several years, consider the impact a major project might have on the tenure decision. On some campuses, a significant and successful commitment to course and program improvement will be viewed very positively. On others, it may be perceived by the tenure committee as significantly detracting from what that faculty member should be doing: research and publishing.

Therefore, before a project begins, it should be discussed with other faculty in the department and top administrators. Find out where priorities are and how this effort will be viewed by those who control the promotion, tenure, and reward systems. In addition, before beginning, make sure administrative support exists for what is being proposed.

Are There Others Who Can Help and Should Be Involved? If there are other faculty who teach the same course or who are directly responsible for the curriculum in which the course is offered, they should be involved or, at least, informed of what is being proposed. Are other faculty willing to assist: faculty who teach the follow-up course, faculty from other departments who send students to the course, faculty with special areas of expertise that could be used?

Do Participants Have Enough Time? The amount of time participating faculty and the support staff have available to use on a project determines not only how soon one can expect to be finished but also how many new materials can be produced. There have been instances where limitations in time and money have necessitated phasing in a new program rather than introducing it all at once.

Should Released Time or Summer Employment Be Used? We have found that it is best to use faculty time during the academic year for design activities and summer employment for the production of materials. That is, if fiscal support for faculty salaries is available, we suggest using summer employment of faculty rather than released time. This recommendation is based on three factors. First, the design phase can usually be completed during the academic year since it does not require an extensive number of hours each week. Because it takes time to collect, analyze, and interpret data, and others will want time to react to the draft designs, meetings scheduled on a once-a-week or twice-a-month basis are fairly common. This provides the team with the necessary time to mull over what has been done and permits revision between meetings. Second, released time arrangements during the academic year rarely provide the faculty with sufficient time to work on the project. During the semester, the faculty given released time often find themselves with additional committee and advisement assignments and meetings that use up the time set aside for the project. During the summer, faculty can schedule the blocks of time they need for writing a student manual, developing instructional materials, and preparing quizzes and exams without interruption for other responsibilities. Third, during the summer, support and production people will usually be more accessible. These three factors make summer employment far more cost effective than released time. Unfortunately, at some institutions this option simply does not exist.

Initiating Projects

As noted in Chapter One, the overall process we are describing covers two major stages: Phase I, project selection and design, and Phase II, production, implementation, and evaluation. When a formal instructional development or support agency is involved, however, we must add two additional early steps: project generation and selection within the design phase.

One of the first problems that an established instructional development unit faces is getting academic departments and faculty to commit themselves to instructional innovation, whereas some faculty or departments may ask the agency for assistance without much encouragement. Most units must find ways to encourage these requests. When considering ways to initiate projects, it is important to maintain balance. If there are very few projects from which to choose, administrative and internal pressures may support those that are low priority or that have little potential for success—an extremely risky business. If, on the other hand, there are too many projects, it may be necessary to refuse or delay even worthwhile projects (and risk alienating faculty) simply because there are not enough resources to provide quality support to all the deserving proposals.

Basically, there are two general approaches for generating projects available to the agency. Each has its own advantages and limitations, and both may, if enough resources exist, be used simultaneously.

The Internal Approach. The staff of the agency either works directly with the central administration, deans, and department chairpersons to identify high-priority needs or reacts to requests made to the unit by interested faculty or by administrators. Little effort is made to sell the services of the agency to the general faculty. Instead, the agency tries to keep a low profile and to support projects that promise maximum impact on the institution. Individual faculty members can, of course, ask for instructional support on their own initiative. However, when this occurs, the chairperson of the department involved and the dean of the school or college should be contacted to explore whether or not the project is of high priority or if the "right" faculty members are involved, and so on. In these instances, before the project is accepted, all efforts are made to ensure that the project has the departmental support it will need to succeed. In this approach, the availability of support dollars is not generally publicized. In the early years of the Center for Instructional Development at Syracuse University, for example, less than 20 percent of the projects were initiated by individual faculty members; most were generated from conversations with chairpersons, academic deans, and the director of the unit. Today, almost all projects are undertaken at the request of deans, department chairpersons, and groups of faculty. At most, one or two major projects a year are initiated by the center's staff who first contact the academic departments. Advantages of the internal approach:

- There is better balance between priorities and projects.
- Fewer projects are rejected.
- The internal approach usually involves teams of faculty that provide broader content expertise and an improved potential for long-term impact.
- The project usually focuses on major instructional elements—courses or curricula.

Disadvantages:

- The overall effort begins slowly and receives little attention.
- The internal approach requires extensive administrative cooperation at both the departmental and college level.

Whether the low profile, which is a posture associated with the internal approach, is an advantage or a disadvantage depends on the campus political situation. If the academic community must know immediately that instructional improvement is being emphasized, then the internal approach would not be appropriate unless it is combined with the external approach.

The External Approach. In this technique, a highly publicized faculty grant program is implemented that encourages individual faculty members to submit proposals for support. The specific scope of support will vary from institution to institution, but the basic concept is generally the same as that found in the early 1970s at Utah State University. The announcement introducing the program to faculty when the program first began was as follows:

President Glen L. Taggart today announced the launching of a Faculty Development Grant Program. As part of the major effort of staff development under way at Utah State University, the program will achieve two purposes: (1) to develop a specific and excellent learning program that will improve student learning at USU and (2) to improve faculty members' instructional skills.

The basic elements of the proposed development program include the following:

1. The university and its colleges will accept a three-month planned project for the improvement of teaching as being a legitimate and desirable full-time assignment for those staff

members interested in an intensive program of instructional improvement.

2. The Instructional Improvement Office of the Learning Resources Program will provide supplementary financial support for space, materials, development, secretarial help, and research help for each appointee.

3. The college and department will provide the resources to release the faculty member for a three-month period within existing policies of the university, college, and department involved.

4. Faculty members who have departmental support will submit proposals to the Advisory Council on Instructional Improvement (ACII) outlining their proposed resident study project and making applications for financial support on a competitive basis. The Office of Instructional Improvement will provide consultant help to staff members in developing proposals if desired.

5. Projects which receive instructional improvement financial support will likely cover a one-year period of time in stages generally outlined as follows:

    -   During the quarter immediately preceding the leave, the staff member will outline his needs, gather data including student inputs, review the literature, visit other classes on and off campus, confer with consultants, and any other activity useful for his program of resident activity.
    -   The next quarter he will be relieved of all teaching and administrative duties and move his office into a study area in the library and spend full time carrying out his improvement of instruction project. He

will receive instructional improvement financial support during this quarter.

- The third quarter the staff member will return to his department and put into operation, field test, and evaluate his developed project as completed.

The above pattern may be modified to fit the needs of individual applications. It is not necessary that a candidate be eligible for a regular sabbatical although this may be one situation. A department can recommend any full-time faculty member or the dean or department head can arrange for his absence during one quarter. It is expected that during the in-residence quarter the staff member will be relieved of all teaching, administrative, and other duties and will work from an office provided by the Improvement of Instruction Office in the Milton R. Merrill Library. The Improvement of Instruction Office will provide consultant help to conceptualize, design, develop, and evaluate the project. The university will consider this activity as a legitimate and desirable method of improving instruction and very valuable to selected staff members who desire to improve their teaching skills.

However, it should be noted that the Utah State University description is far more definite about the five specific stages of the project than the announcements found in most institutions. Most schools using this approach also prepare a specific project proposal outline for faculty. This technique not only assures the selection committee that they will have the information they need to make their decisions, it also helps the development process itself by making the faculty think through their problems and potential solutions before they submit their proposals.

The State University College at Brockport, New York, added an interesting section to its proposal form called Departmental Commitment. This section represented a specific attempt to generate long-term departmental commitments for each project and thus solve the problem of "short-term" project life found on many campuses. The general announcement used at Brockport also included a very clear and essential statement on copyright policy that covers all materials produced as part of the project. A small grant program instituted at Syracuse University with the support of the Lilly Endowment, Inc., and later carried on by the university followed this same approach with the application, requiring that formal letters demonstrating departmental and deans' support be included with the proposal. The rating criteria that were used emphasized this requirement and also weighed heavily the impact the project would have on students. Advantages of the external approach:

- The external approach generates many project requests.
- It is an excellent method of advertising administrative commitment to instructional improvement.

Disadvantages:

- Many proposed projects will be low priority and may be of questionable quality.
- Faculty who are turned down may be antagonized.
- Close control of projects may be lost unless specific operational guidelines and controls are built into the funding process.
- Coordination of projects to meet specific institution-wide goals may be limited.
- Political considerations for institutional balance or the particular makeup of the selection committee may result in the awarding of grants to some high-risk, low-priority projects.
- Most projects involve a single faculty member, thus limiting the project's potential for long-term continuance.
- Projects tend to be limited in scope (units or parts of courses), having, therefore, modest impact.

If quality is to be maintained when the external approach is used, the control of every project should be placed with the development unit rather than with the requesting department. On campuses at which funds have been given directly to the department, results have often been unsatisfactory. On at least one campus, the funds were actually transferred to the department budget and used for other purposes. For maximum success, both institutional commitment to the project and quality control throughout are required.

A Note of Caution. Whether the internal or external approach is used, there will be times when faculty involved in course or curriculum improvement efforts will, despite the availability of support, neither seek nor accept assistance. In some instances, particularly in course-related projects, the faculty member will feel, sometimes correctly, that he or she can do it alone and no help is needed. Successful projects have been and will continue to be done by faculty working independently who simply work better on their own.

In curriculum projects, the reasons for not accepting or even avoiding assistance are often more complex. In some instances, the faculty simply do not want someone from outside the department to see the problems that they are having. These may be interpersonal or discipline-related. Some faculty may feel they need no help or that only someone in the discipline could possibly be of assistance. Occasionally, the faculty may not realize the complexity of what they are undertaking and perceive the process as simple and easy. The administrator of the program may feel responsible for many of the problems and may not want an outsider, particularly another administrator, to see what is going on.

There is little question that, in most instances, the involvement of support staff would improve the quality of the product and the efficiency of its completion. However, support personnel must realize that no matter how much they might be able to assist, they may not always be asked to provide help, no matter how significant the problem is. It is extremely frustrating at times to see problems arise that could have been avoided, but a support staff has no choice. A support unit is only effective when the faculty have *invited* its staff into the project. Administrative "lay-on"—that is, "you *will* use this unit"—simply doesn't work.

All the agency can do is explain to the faculty what services it provides and how it operates and suggest that the potential clients talk to others with whom the agency has worked. The next move must be up to the faculty.

Selecting the Project

Two overriding factors should determine whether or not a project is to be undertaken: the project must meet the academic priorities established for the institution, and there should be good reasons to believe it will succeed. One of the paradoxes of instructional development is that those projects most easily undertaken often have little to do with the established goals or needs of the academic department or institution and are, therefore, highly questionable for support and investment.

Establishing Academic Priorities. Realistic priorities for instructional development are established from data collected from a number of sources: society (the community), students, the instructional staff, and the administration.

What programs should be emphasized and improved? Where do problems exist? What changes are needed, and are they possible under the existing structure? Can and should fundamental restructuring be encouraged?

It is critical that in establishing priorities all those who are or should be concerned are involved. Their participation is particularly important at the individual and community levels where specific subgroups are often overlooked.

Although much has yet to be learned about how best to identify and describe an institution's academic needs and priorities, needs assessment can be extremely useful at this point in considering the following four groups: students, society, faculty, and administration.

Students can provide excellent input into the value and effectiveness of academic programs. Unfortunately, structured attempts to gather these data are the exception. Although in many instances only the more politically active, highly capable student is heard, it is important to seek input from *all* segments of the student population, including minority and international students. Quite often the students' immediate needs, as they see them, must be met before efforts to meet their long-term and more significant needs can be undertaken. In effect, different groups may require different objectives, procedures, and instructional elements. Are there certain courses in which dropout or failure rates are high? Are the better students leaving certain programs? Where are enrollments dropping? These are all key questions in identifying problem areas.

What are the needs of the society in which the educational program exists? These may be on a national or a local level or specific to the particular population a professional program is designed to serve. A university serving a rural area and one in an urban center would probably have some goals that are identical but others that reflect the differences between their locations.

How should the academic program be designed to function when the student population is highly transient? Junior colleges located near military establishments and in the inner city, for example, can expect to face an even greater challenge because of the high mobility of their students. Such problems must be identified because they have a direct effect on the priorities and program design of instructional systems.

The educational system must also consider the future needs of the society. For example, it must anticipate the skills that will be required by the time today's freshmen graduate and look for employment. All too often we have designed our institutions to meet immediate needs without giving enough attention to long-range requirements. With sufficient effort, trends toward change can be identified. In the early 1970s, for example, the demand for graduate engineers, as well as for experts in certain fields of science and education, decreased, while law, medicine, management, and architecture programs were all undergoing expansion on many campuses. As a result, we now find overexpansion in these fields, with other fields demanding far more trained personnel than are available. These trends could have been anticipated, yet few academic programs showed any related modification in the scope of their programs or in the number of students enrolled.

Recently, some effort has been made on a few campuses to

establish a close working relationship between the academic departments and those who hire their graduates. At Syracuse, for example, boards of visitors have been established for each professional school to provide input and open doors to resources that help all the parties involved. The Center for Instructional Development has found that advisory groups for projects in the professional areas not only help to identify a need for revision of existing programs but, during the design process, they provide excellent suggestions for what should be included. Another spin-off has been the willingness of those serving on these advisory groups to make available to the programs student internships and other resources.

The instructional staff can provide information about problems in the present system and about changed emphasis in areas of knowledge. Major discoveries, new theories, and discipline modifications should be considered because of their impact on priorities. Are the faculty unhappy with what exists and, if so, why? When major problems exist, the faculty are usually aware of them.

It is often helpful to involve faculty in other schools or departments. The expertise, for example, of management specialists can be used to help design academic programs in school administration or political science; psychologists can be helpful in programs in mass communication; and some faculty from law schools have expertise that can be most useful in designing a course in advertising. In some instances, we have found that the faculty in one school already have courses available that meet important needs of another. What problems do other faculty see? How do these concerns relate to the project under discussion?

A central administration that is sensitive to the concerns of parents, alumni, students, and faculty and that is aware of both budget and resource limitations can often identify the specific academic programs that need the most attention. The priorities it establishes for the institution are directly affected by the availability of human and material resources. For example, if dollars become scarce, programs may have to be reduced or eliminated; likewise, the number of students and amount of available space can influence the educational process.

Since significant demographic changes are usually prominent and readily diagnosed, they are likely to generate easily articulated goals. Moreover, unless care is taken, there is a danger that new job-related objectives will displace the broader, less easily defined general but essential ("liberal") goals of education. To prevent this from happening, the broader, long-range needs must be kept in mind whenever priorities are reordered. This is an important responsibility of the academic administrators.

Administrators can expect agreement only on the need for change, not on specific changes themselves. Students, for example, may stress modifications in the course content or in the quality of instruction, but faculty may recommend that less able and poorly prepared students be dropped. These differences make value judgments difficult. But solutions to problems uncovered do not have to be found at this stage in the process. It is essential to identify only the key questions and problems that will have to be resolved if a project is implemented. This information is needed in developing priorities.

Final Selection. Once needs and priorities have been established and articulated, the responsibility of the development staff is to work closely with the central administration, the deans, and heads of departments to identify and implement projects that will help to reach these goals.

The final decision as to whether to undertake a specific project must involve both those requesting that the work be done and those that must do the work. If the necessary elements are not available, projects started by administrative fiat can prove to be far more damaging than the problems they were designed to solve. Regardless of the priority of a project, there are times when it would be a mistake to begin instructional development. Agency personnel responsible for project selection should consider fully the risks involved.

For maximum potential, the following elements should exist.

1. A solid base of instructional talent must be available. Without a quality teaching staff with both successful classroom experience and discipline expertise, the project will never

develop the essential academic respectability. Outside expertise can be used, but consultants cannot provide specific teaching skills and knowledge of content required.

2. There must be instructional stability. Beginning a project is unwise if the school or department involved is undergoing major curriculum revision or has a history of administrative instability with the chairperson's or dean's position vacant or recently filled. Under such circumstances, a decision about curriculum redesign made today, no matter how valid, may be overruled tomorrow. Unfortunately, highly successful projects on several campuses have been lost when a new department chairperson arrived. Interested in establishing his or her own program, the chairperson canceled the existing program by administrative fiat without extensive research into why it was undertaken and what effects it had.

3. More than one faculty member should be involved, and those who do participate should command the respect of their peers; a departmental support base for the project is essential. While it is sometimes impossible to avoid, designing a project around a single faculty member can be risky. Quite often development projects become associated with an individual and, despite the quality of the program, can terminate when that faculty member is promoted or leaves (a common event with talented people). Involving a team of faculty not only will provide the project with a stronger academic base but also will help build in long-range project durability. One must assume that the more talented the faculty, the greater the possibility of promotion and other job offers. Since there is usually an attempt to involve the best teachers possible in these projects, this advancement seems to be the rule rather than the exception.

4. The anticipated time to completion must be realistic. It is imperative that the support staff understand how soon the faculty and department expect implementation. If, for political reasons, rapid results are required, limit projects to those that utilize a greater proportion of existing materials and thus take less time for development. Most projects

involving the redesign of one or more courses require a minimum of eighteen months for development before their field testing is completed; others that are equally important but require less production and fewer new materials can be implemented in far less time. For example, the version of the Syracuse University Freshman English Composition course used in the 1970s was fully implemented for 100 students in less than three months after development began. An extremely efficient faculty and the combination of previously field-tested techniques and materials made this possible. A self-paced, twelve-credit calculus sequence was implemented in almost the same amount of time; however, in this instance the course began before all the new instructional materials were completed. For most projects, however, a slower, more deliberate sequence is necessary. A new introductory economics course, for example, took over two years before the entire program was fully implemented.

Not all projects that are supported can be expected to meet every one of these criteria. Both operational and political concerns can delay the most ideal project or can place high priority on projects that have little chance of success or that will impact only a few students. For example, support might be provided for a project of otherwise low priority because it might represent a major breakthrough in a school or department; that is, such support might be the first foot in the door of a department or school that, despite existing problems, has been hostile to development. If, in a campus-wide project, there is an imbalance between the size and importance of programs and the support that is provided, adjustments in program support are often necessary. In addition, chief administrators or deans may, based on their highest priorities, request support of one program over another while clearly understanding the risk involved.

If an open grant approach (external) is used, many of these concerns cannot be realistically taken into consideration. Selection is, for the most part, out of administrators' hands when an awards committee is involved. Finally, particularly when the program is successful, there are occasions when the development, evaluation, or production units are simply unable to take on another project because of existing commitments. When this happens, it may be necessary to delay the start of a program or to develop it more slowly.

While the conditions that threaten the success of a project cannot always be avoided, they must be kept in mind throughout the selection process.

In summary, one should try to avoid

- Projects in which the academic expertise is lacking (Remember, the developer is a facilitator, not a content expert.)
- Departments or schools that are in the process of changing administrators
- Projects that involve only one faculty member
- Projects that do not have a strong support base in the department in which they are undertaken
- Projects in which what is expected is unrealistic in terms of time and existing resources

Problems and failures are inevitable, but proper project selection can substantially reduce the probability of both. The following outline is a suggested sequence for selecting projects.

1. **Is the project needed?** (Statements of need and general priorities from both formal and informal sources)
   Student statements, failure rate/attrition, enrollment.
   Faculty statements.
   Community statements/employment history of graduates.
   If successful, how significant is the impact?
2. **Is the academic area stable?**
   Is the program stable?
   Are key administrative changes under way?
   Are faculty changes under way?
   Are curriculum revisions under way?
   Is there potential for long-range growth?
   Enrollment patterns.

National needs assessment.
National trends and governmental directions.
3. **What is the potential for success?**
    Does the dean's office support the project?
    Is departmental commitment available (faculty and chair-
        person)?
    Are sufficient qualified faculty available?
    Is the project at the beginning of the curriculum sequence?
    Is the time frame realistic to reach goals?
    Will the faculty involved follow required/recommended
        procedures?
4. **Does the agency have the necessary resources available?**
    What commitment is required (staff, production, budget,
        and so on)?
    Is staff available?
    Can the time frame be met or can it be modified?
    If necessary, can the scope of the project be modified?
5. **Are there political factors that should be considered?** (Are
    there times when, despite high risks or potentially modest
    returns, a project should be undertaken anyway?)
    Where does the project fall within the priorities of indi-
        vidual schools or departments?
    Does the project represent a breakthrough with the school,
        department, or key individual?
    How does the project affect university-wide program
        balance?
    Does the project have priority with top administrators?

    After reviewing the factors, one option for action must be
taken. The project selection committee may choose from the
following options:

*   Full support
*   Support with fewer resources or slow down the development
    process
*   No support
*   Support with all those concerned aware of the high risk
    involved

Note: If key factors change during the design process, the decision to support should be reconsidered and possibly modified.

Once a project is selected for implementation, it must be treated as a whole. The project cannot be separated into units or segments during the design phase, which will be described in Chapters Four and Five. Remember, the more carefully you select projects, the greater the chance of success and significant impact.

3

Selecting a Design Team and Establishing Goals and Procedures

This chapter focuses on getting a project under way. The initial design meeting is described with a discussion of who should participate and what should be accomplished.

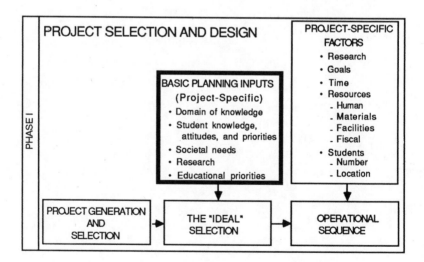

Overview

While a number of conversations must take place prior to the start of a project, the first formal meeting of those who will actively participate in the project is extremely important. At this meeting, the overall goals of the project are established, the development procedures are described, the roles of all the participants are defined, and the fundamental groundwork for the project is laid. Basic institutional procedures and guidelines are also reviewed at this meeting.

Who Should Be Involved

The meeting should include the instructional developer (serving as chair) and all the faculty who will be working directly on the project. A team of faculty, when possible, is always preferred, since it provides a stronger academic base. If a particular course is the focus of the project, an effort should be made to include all faculty who teach it. In curriculum projects, the team should consist of carefully selected representatives from each of the major academic programs or departments involved. On any team, one faculty member should be identified as the key content expert and coordinator. This individual will be responsible for directing and coordinating those activities that take place within the academic department when neither the instructional developer nor the evaluator is present.

If the group is large (over eight or so), a small steering committee is suggested. If the group is too large, it becomes impossible to set up meetings and the efficiency of the group suffers. The people on the committee will be expected to participate very actively in the development process. In some instances, key administrators (deans or department chairpersons) will also wish to participate and should be encouraged to do so. The selection of this committee is so important to a successful project that it should be given careful thought and, on occasion, extensive deliberation.

The academic team leader should have the ability, the respect, and the content expertise needed to coordinate the efforts of other faculty members. In some instances, the team leader has been a department chair who wished to be actively involved in the design process.

Using Graduate Students. Although graduate students have, at times, been members of the development team, it is important to view them as support for the project and not rely on them to play a major role. Experience has shown that delegating content decisions to graduate students sets a project up for negative reaction when the design is presented to faculty for adoption. As noted earlier, key faculty must be involved whenever possible and must have ownership in the project from the beginning. While faculty may enjoy the thought of delegating some of the work, they do not happily delegate content decisions; and, in designing for the ideal, their academic backgrounds and experience are necessary.

Evaluation Assistance. Since demographic data about the students and, when appropriate, the professional field are often topics at this initial meeting, having a person there who can handle the collection and interpretation of this information is most useful. Attendance at this meeting by an evaluation specialist (if one is available) also provides to the group an additional range of expertise while permitting this evaluator to have a better understanding of a project as it gets under way. This early participation also helps those who will work together later in the project to get to know one another.

Preplanning to Completion

Laying the Groundwork. Before the first formal design meeting of the whole team, prior meetings must be held with key faculty and administrators. These meetings help to establish priorities, determine the scope of the project, and identify who should be involved, the resources available, and the procedures that will be followed. These early preproject meetings can also help to develop the commitment that will be required from the department and the faculty. In some instances, these earlier meetings may stop a project that should not have been begun.

Goals. To be successful, the initial design meeting must achieve several important objectives.

1. The goals and scope of the project and the anticipated time line should be reviewed and agreed upon.
2. At the conclusion of the initial design meeting, those participating must be comfortable with what will follow and have a clear understanding of what they will be responsible for.
3. Everyone involved should understand that the role of the instructional developer is that of a process person, helping the participating faculty get through the development process by asking questions, playing the devil's advocate, and offering suggestions.
4. At the conclusion of the meeting, there must be a commitment to get things under way so that everyone feels that progress has taken place.

In some instances it is possible, by the end of the first meeting, to have developed the initial draft of at least part of an ideal program. We have found it effective at the end of this initial meeting to have the developer review what has been accomplished and then send the summary to participants for comments and reaction.

In addition, other basics should be covered at this meeting. These range from a review of the institution's copyright policy (see Resource A) to the establishment of meeting times, roles and responsibilities, deadlines, and so on, and whether or not released time or summer employment opportunities will be available for faculty.

Case Study: An Orientation Program for Teaching Assistants. In the summer of 1986, a decision was made by Syracuse University's vice-president for undergraduate studies, Ronald Cavanagh, and the vice-president for research and graduate affairs, Karen Hiiemae, to explore the possibility of implementing a required orientation program for all new teaching assistants. The key first step was establishing a steering committee and appointing to this committee those individuals who would be essential for designing, implementing, and supporting any program that might be proposed. Since this project would, if it was going to be successful, involve faculty, administrators, and graduate students, the committee that was established had the following members (in addition to the two vice-presidents who served as co-chairs).

- The director of the graduate school
- Two faculty representatives who were responsible for the training and supervision of teaching assistants in their departments (Faculty from English and mathematics, departments with the largest number of teaching assistants, were selected.)
- Two graduate students, including the president of the Graduate Student Organization
- A faculty representative of the graduate council
- The director of the Center for Instructional Development, who would be responsible for the overall design of the program

Once a decision was made to implement the program that was later proposed, the steering committee was expanded to include a representative from the unit that provided support to international students, the Office of International Service, and the two individuals who would manage the program. Several additional support staff attended all meetings.

In retrospect, it is clear that the planning that went into the selection of this key group was not wasted. By the conclusion of the first advisory committee meeting, several task forces had been established, recommendations for membership had been made, responsibilities had been defined, and a schedule for future meetings had been set up. Every committee member was to play an essential role in the successful design and implementation of this program. Two of the faculty members assumed responsibility for important elements of the program, the graduate students were to play major roles in both the design and implementation of both training and social activities, and the graduate school developed a number of administrative procedures that were essential for a smooth-running program.

Summary

Care must be taken in identifying individuals who must be involved from the beginning of a program and in establishing the committees and task forces that will be responsible for the project once a decision to move ahead is made. The initial design meeting should help everyone involved to understand what they are being asked to do and the time that will most likely be required for them to accomplish their task. A checklist of who should participate and what should be covered in this initial design meeting follows.

1. Participants
   - Faculty for course projects—all with major teaching/ administrative responsibilities (maximum 4–6); faculty for curriculum projects—representatives of all major academic areas
   - Administrator(s)—dean or department chair (optional)
   - Instructional developer (chairs meeting)
   - Evaluator (optional)
   - Graduate assistants (staff role only)
2. Topics to be covered
   - Need for and general goals of project (review)
   - Review of development (design model)
   - Roles of participants (required time commitment)
   - Available resources (including stipends for faculty)
   - Anticipated time lines
   - Significant institutional policies and procedures (including royalty and copyright)
   - Schedule for future meetings
   - Initiating work on design of program

4

Gathering
and Analyzing
Essential Data

This chapter presents a review of those questions that should be asked and the data that should be collected as work on the design of a course or curriculum begins. Several case studies are included.

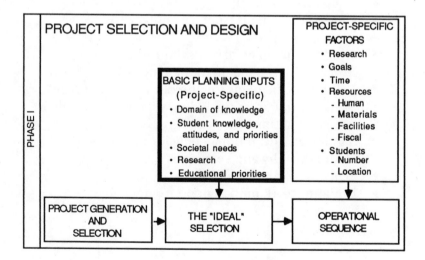

Overview

Once the decision has been made to begin a specific project, basic data must be collected in five areas as you begin to work on the actual design of the program: (1) the characteristics of the students—their backgrounds, abilities, and priorities; (2) the desires and needs of the society; (3) the educational priorities of the institution, school, or department; (4) the domain of knowledge that is appropriate to the scope of the project; and (5) related research. Surveys and achievement tests, as well as informal discussion sessions held specifically for this purpose, may be used at this point to gather information. The data collected at this point in these five areas are extremely important since they help to define required and optional elements of the program, determine if remedial units or exemptions are appropriate, and form the basis for selecting basic content and determining instructional objectives.

Student Inputs

An important source of data that is often overlooked is the student. If the program is to be instructionally effective, those involved must, as they design it, be sensitive to student data.

Student Entry Level (Knowledge of Subject)

Surprising as it may seem, it is the rare faculty member who is aware of what entering students actually know about the subject and can be sure that the assumptions made about prerequisites are accurate. More commonly, faculty overestimate skills, prior knowledge, and competencies rather than underestimate them. Studies by Pervin and Rubin (1967), Dresser (1971), and others have suggested that insensitivity to students' backgrounds, interests, and needs is a primary reason that many students feel dissatisfied with or leave their institutions. Faculty assume that their students have the prerequisites that their courses require. This gap between what is expected and what actually exists has proven especially significant in the areas of reading, writing, basic mathematics, and specialized science vocabularies. Some students fail science because they cannot handle simple mathematical problems. Others have difficulty in history and social science because their working vocabularies are smaller than the text presumes.

In studies undertaken at Syracuse University, for example, we have found that some students who can pass calculus tests have problems at the eighth-grade level with multiplication and division of fractions, decimals, and percents or with word problems. On many campuses, as many as 50 percent of the entering students have significant problems in at least one of these areas. The vocabulary level of many textbooks is, unfortunately, appropriate for students several years older than the intended readers. This is complicated by the fact that the standard texts used in many introductory courses have actually become more difficult and complex as they have moved from edition to edition (Burstyn and Santa, 1977). Data about what entering students know and do not know are important components of designing ideal programs.

These data are also useful for estimating the number of students who will need remedial and review assignments and the number who enter a program with some of the objectives already met and thus warrant exemptions and/or options, perhaps for additional credit. The problem of entering students who already meet certain course objectives is becoming more and more prevalent as traditional elements of the college curriculum are taught earlier in the educational process. For example, it is not unusual to find parts of college-level courses taught in high school or high school materials taught in junior high school classrooms. One recent Syracuse University survey found that approximately 20 percent of the students in an introductory psychology course had had formal instruction in the subject while in high school. An additional 2 percent had been able to take college psychology courses at a nearby institution while still in the eleventh or twelfth grade. The immediate problem created by such variance in the entering levels of students faces many faculty, who discover that while they have underestimated the competencies of some students, they have, in the same course, overestimated the abilities of others.

Attitudes

The attitudes that students have toward a particular course or field of study can influence what they learn. If they are initially hostile to a subject, learning will suffer unless attitudes can be changed. As a result, it is vital that we take student attitudes into account when we design a course and modify the program by incorporating new materials or by adding new options. Students who enroll in science courses for nonscience majors, for example, may dislike the science even before they begin the course. If this attitude is taken into account when the course is designed and appropriate steps are taken, a positive attitude toward science can be developed in many of the students.

In some instances, entering students may see little value in the knowledge and skills taught in a course. To produce the attitude necessary to improve student performance, the content of the course can be related to the interests of the student; at least some attempt must be made to explain why the course is important. The newness of a course can satisfactorily maintain a student's interest for only a limited time.

A study at one institution, which shall remain anonymous for obvious reasons, showed that before its redesign, one physics course had been having a definite effect on the attitudes of the students. Students usually entered the course with a somewhat neutral attitude toward the discipline, but, by the time the course was completed, their attitude had become completely hostile! In this instance, the faculty had assumed these were highly motivated science majors, while what they had, in fact, were several hundred liberal arts students who wanted a science course that met Mondays, Wednesdays, and Fridays at 10 A.M., and this was the only one that had available space in it at the time they registered.

Attitudinal data can be extremely useful in helping to develop an effective instructional sequence.

Priorities and Expectations

What do the students expect from a course, and what are their priorities as they relate to the area of study? If the students' expectations and priorities do not agree with initial content, there must be either new units added early in the program to modify their expectations and priorities or new content built into the program that meets or modifies their anticipation. Data on what a student expects can often be enlightening to a teacher. For example, a Syracuse University survey in an American history course showed that the students were far more interested in the American Revolution and in the American Indian than had been anticipated. Assignments in these areas were easily expanded without changing the overall goals of the course. The survey identified excellent topics for optional assignments and required papers.

Long-Range Goals

An analysis of the long-range goals of students and their major fields of interest can also help to identify special seminars, options, and projects that might be included in a course. At the same time, such an analysis also can help to relate the course content more closely to areas and topics that particularly interest students. The interrelationship of separate disciplines can have a direct and positive effect on the attitudes of students toward a course that might otherwise be perceived as being unrelated and uninteresting.

A general mathematics course, for example, can have seminars or special projects relating to history (the role of mathematics in history), modern music (new mathematics-based notation techniques), and business (use of statistics). The opera portion of a general music course with a large enrollment of history and political science majors could include a discussion of the role of opera in history and politics, and the more general areas of art, history, music, religion, and literature can often be interrelated. For example, why is the music, art, or literature of a given period the way that it is? This question cannot be answered without studying the politics, religion, and history of the period and of the place. The following case studies illustrate the importance of basic information collection in determining program changes for introductory courses.

Case Studies

An Introductory Course in Religion. In this project, a survey instrument was prepared and distributed to a sample of students enrolled in the existing introductory course the semester before work was scheduled to begin (see Exhibit 1). The instrument was intended to identify the levels of interest and understanding that students could be expected to bring to the new course that would replace an existing course. The items included in the instrument were developed jointly by evaluation specialists and faculty from the Department of Religion. When responses had been collected and tabulated, the students' intentions were viewed in the context of the faculty's expectations.

The data generated by this instrument (see Table 1) resulted in significant changes in the intended course design. These data not only had a significant impact on the design of the course, but also allowed us to anticipate, fairly accurately, the number of students who would later enroll in different options.

The value of this instrument to the project is best described by a faculty member who, at this time, served as the course coordinator for the department: "The test instrument employed in the development of experimental Religion 105 was designed to indicate what patterns, if any, of student interest, disinterest, expectation, recognition, or dislike would be likely to characterize a typical population involved in this course. The results of the application of this instrument at first appeared so ambiguous as to be useless. Under continuing consideration, however, they proved most helpful.

"While initial analysis showed no clear pattern of interest for any particular subject matter, or issue, or method in the

**Exhibit 1. Selection of Items Taken from a Survey of
Student Interest Levels in Religion.**

The following list contains topics that could be included in this course. Rate
each topic according to your level of *interest* in it. Use the following scale.

A	B	C	D
No interest at all	A little interest	Moderate interest	Very high interest

1. Women's lib and mythologies of creation.
2. Ecology and creation stories.
3. Psychotherapy and mystical experience.
4. The problem of a good God and the existence of evil in the world.
5. Science and religion.
6. Abortion and the church.
7. Pacifism and the holy wars of Judaism, Christianity, and Islam.
8. Sex and an absolutist ethic.
9. Number symbolism in the problem of the Trinity.
10. Technology as a new religion.
11. Apocalypticism and progress.
12. Modern mythologies of the creative hero.
13. The death of God in ancient religions.
14. The religious history of the future.
15. Should churches be taxed?
16. The artist as the religious hero of our time.
17. God as relative rather than absolute.
18. Is Zen possible in the West?
19. Yoga and drugs.
20. Traditional religions and the occult.
21. The religion of the American Indian and paleface Christianity.
22. The end of religion.
23. Polytheism in our time.
24. Modern pantheons.
25. Dreams and religion.
26. The poetry of the Bible.
27. Ballad and rock music as scripture.
28. Job and psychology.
29. Jesus freaks—then and now.
30. Witchcraft.
31. Capitalism in church and synagogue.
32. Communes and religion.
33. The birth and death of religious institutions.
34. Are there other topics in religion of interest to you that are not listed here? Please list them on the back of your answer sheet.

Table 1. Rated Levels of Interest for Possible Topics in Religion ($N = 100$).

HIGH INTEREST
Percentage of students who judged their interest in the topic to be "moderate" or "very high"

Psychotherapy and mystical experience.	63%
Abortion and the church.	58%
Sex and an absolutist ethic.	60%
Is Zen possible in the West?	57%
Yoga and drugs.	53%
Traditional religions and the occult.	56%
The end of religion.	65%
Dreams and religion.	60%
Witchcraft.	70%

LOW INTEREST
Percentage of students who judged their interest in the topic to be "little" or "none at all"

Number symbolism in the problem of the Trinity.	62%
Apocalypticism and progress.	71%
Should churches be taxed?	62%
Modern pantheons.	82%
The poetry of the Bible.	61%
Capitalism in church and synagogue.	57%

OTHERS

Women's lib and mythologies of creation.
Ecology and creation stories.
The problem of a good God and the existence of evil in the world.
Science and religion.
Pacifism and the holy wars of Judaism, Christianity, and Islam.
Technology as a new religion.
Modern mythologies of the creative hero.
The death of God in ancient religions.
The religious history of the future.
The artist as the religious hero of our time.
God as relative rather than absolute.
The religion of the American Indian and paleface Christianity.
Polytheism in our time.
Ballad and rock music as scripture.
Job and psychology.
Jesus freaks — then and now.
Communes and religion.
The birth and death of religious institutions.

study of religion, it did reveal a wide variety of levels of recognition as well as diverse preferences for formats of presentation. We concluded initially that the instrument had not given us specific or helpful information about subject matter, issue, format, and so on. What we later came to see was that the concern for diversity, for flexibility, for variety of instructional formats was specifically the pattern that was common to the sample population. The test instrument clearly suggested modular construction and a flexible selection procedure. It also became apparent that a common base of meaning and of definitions had to be developed before the course could be effectively taught."

When revising an existing course or curriculum, collect data from a representative sample of students before work begins on a project. Such data can provide, as they did in the religion course, extremely useful information.

Microeconomics. As in the case of the religion course, an existing economics course permitted faculty to collect important data from students as the department undertook redesign of the introductory course. These data had significant impact on the objectives of the revised program, on the materials that were developed, and on the perceptions of the faculty member: "Several student concerns were clearly expressed in the data we collected for our survey. Two in particular were to have a major impact on my thinking as I worked through the redesign of the course: First, the lack of coordination the students found between the textbook and the lectures and, second, the lack of competency among some of the teaching assistants with respect to course content. The student manuals we developed were, in fact, specifically designed to resolve these problems. By setting forth objectives for each unit of the course, the manual establishes a common foundation of course content across all sections of the course. The inclusion of questions on the textbook readings that highlight the issues specified by these objectives provide my students with a clear correlation between the text and the lectures."

Societal Inputs

The second major area of data collection is information that is obtained from outside the institution: from alumni, employers, recruiters, and published reports and research. While most data of this type are related to and collected for specific programs, there have been instances in which the information has been more generalized and could have a direct bearing on a number of programs. An example has been our effort to identify the knowledge, skills, and understanding that each student should have prior to graduation.

Over the past several years, staff of the Center for Instructional Development reviewed the literature and interviewed and surveyed employers, recruiters, faculty, and alumni in many fields to identify those skills and knowledge that are basic for success. This information was then used by faculty as they developed their own courses and curricula. In addition to the list of specific skills and competencies that was developed, three observations should be made.

1. Regardless of the discipline and whether the list was developed from a review of the literature or by faculty, alumni, recruiters, or employers in the United States or in other countries, final lists were almost identical.
2. More and more employers were saying, "Give us the well-rounded individual, the generalist (with good basic competencies). . . we'll provide the specialized training." In other words, they were asking for the liberal arts graduate. (Unfortunately, while the leaders were saying this, we often found that recruiters for the same companies were still focusing on the narrower skills and proficiencies.)
3. While our focus was primarily on basic skills, it should be noted that, in addition to an understanding of history, an appreciation of the arts and humanities and a knowledge of government and of the responsibilities of the individual in the society were identified as fundamental goals of any educational system.

More specifically, eight basic survival skills appeared regularly in the literature and on the lists that were developed when respondents were asked to identify which skills or competencies every student should have upon graduation.

1. *Effective communication:* the ability to write, speak, and listen effectively
2. *Interpersonal skills:* the ability to work well with others in both leadership and support roles
3. *Interviewing skills:* the ability to handle an interview situation effectively
4. *Functional mathematics:* the ability to solve fraction, decimal, percent, and word problems
5. *Basic managerial finance:* the skills of personal accounting, understanding budgets, and so on
6. *Problem solving and decision making:* making the right decision in complex situations in which some action is required
7. *Resource utilization:* the ability to, first, identify what you need to know and, second, know where to get your answer
8. *Computer utilization:* an understanding of what a computer can do for you and then how to use this technology to meet your own specific needs

Not only can community sources identify competencies required for success in a field, but they can also provide insight into whether or not these instructional goals are being met.

A 1984 report, *Future Trends in Broadcast Journalism*, describes a study conducted by the Radio-Television News Directors Association in which radio and television news directors and faculty in related professional programs were asked to identify those skills that "on-air" people required and then to evaluate recent graduates on the skills that were considered important.

For on-air people in television, four qualities were identified as being particularly important: writing skills, the ability to communicate well on the air, the ability to think clearly, and the ability to work under tight deadlines (Table 2). More than 80 percent also identified interviewing skills (the ability to effectively interview others) as very important.

Significant problems were uncovered when this study began to compare what was needed to the competencies they were finding in those who were applying for positions.

Not only were recent graduates rated low on each of the

Table 2. Importance of Various Skills for On-Air People (*N* = 112).

	Very Important (%)	Somewhat Important (%)	Not Very Important (%)	Don't Know/ No Answer (%)
Writing skills	96.4	2.7	0.0	0.9
Ability to communicate well on the air	96.4	3.6	0.0	0.0
Ability to think clearly	96.4	3.6	0.0	0.0
Ability to work under tight deadlines	92.0	7.1	0.9	0.0
Interviewing skills	83.9	14.3	0.9	0.9
Creativity and ability to approach stories from unusual angles	67.0	28.6	4.5	0.0
Knowledge of how government operates	66.1	29.5	2.7	1.8
Understanding of human behavior	55.4	44.6	0.0	0.0
Understanding of history	50.0	47.3	2.7	0.0
Editing skills	28.6	50.0	19.6	1.8
Ability to handle broadcasting equipment	21.4	50.0	28.6	0.0
Understanding of art and culture	18.8	61.6	18.8	0.9

Source: Future Trends in Broadcast Journalism, 1984, p. 39.

twelve categories, but they were rated lowest on the very skills considered most important: writing, the ability to work under tight deadlines, and the ability to communicate well on the air (Table 3).

The writers of the report also found that the university professors tended to be far more generous in the assessment of their graduates than were the professionals in the field. The majority of faculty, unlike the professionals in the field, stated that entry-level people could write very well and had the ability to work under tight deadlines.

Unfortunately, the findings of this report are not unique. Recruiters and employers have consistently reported that, while the college graduates they interview or hire have the content

Table 3. Evaluation of Recent Graduates on Skills Considered Important.
(Based in each case on news directors who consider the skill
at least somewhat important)

	Rate Very Well (%)	Somewhat (%)	Not Very (%)	Don't Know/ No Answer (%)
Ability to handle broad- casting equipment (73)*	8.2	61.6	27.4	2.7
Editing skills (77)	5.2	46.8	46.8	1.3
Writing skills (99)	2.0	29.3	68.7	0.0
Ability to work under tight deadlines (99)	3.0	40.4	53.5	3.0
Ability to think clearly (100)	5.0	67.0	26.0	2.0
Creativity and ability to approach stories from unusual angles (97)	4.1	51.5	42.3	2.1
Understanding of human behavior (100)	5.0	53.0	41.0	1.0
Knowledge of how govern- ment operates (95)	3.2	41.1	54.7	1.1
Understanding of history (98)	3.1	43.9	50.0	3.1
Interviewing skills (98)	2.0	50.0	46.9	1.0
Understanding of art and culture (80)	3.8	53.7	36.2	6.3
Ability to communicate well on the air (100)	1.0	46.0	52.0	1.0

* Each figure in parentheses represents the number of those who say the skill is at least somewhat important.
Source: *Future Trends in Broadcast Journalism,* 1984, p. 39.

expertise of their respective disciplines, few can write or speak effectively.

Discipline-Specific Information. While some of the data collected from community sources are general, an equal amount are discipline-specific. For example, in a project re-designing the music education program, most of our graduates told us that sometime in their careers they were required to design an auditorium or a classroom for teaching and playing music — a task for which they felt they were totally unprepared. A unit on facilities design and equipment selection has now been added to the curriculum.

In another survey, major retailers identified specific math skills as a major problem and indicated that a significant increase in the use of computers in the field was likely. These data had a direct impact on the retailing curriculum that was developed. This curriculum project of the College of Human Development provides an interesting example of the application of societal and student surveys. The project is currently under way.

Case Study: College for Human Development. Questionnaires are extremely effective tools for collecting discipline-specific information. Recently, staff of the Center for Instructional Development assisted the faculty and dean of Syracuse University's College for Human Development in reviewing their four major undergraduate programs. The instruments that were developed for distribution to students, faculty, and alumni were somewhat unusual in that they were designed to serve two distinct purposes: first, to provide general information, and second, to provide discipline-specific data focusing on particular programs and majors. While the general questions were developed jointly with a steering committee, the discipline-specific sections were the product of extensive conversations with the faculty of each of the three major divisions, focusing specifically on the information that faculty felt would be most useful in helping them to evaluate and improve their programs.

The result was a questionnaire that had the following sections.

1. Professional skills and personal skills
2. Discipline-specific competencies—what should be included in an undergraduate program
3. View of future
4. Individual background information

While sections 1, 3, and 4 were identical for all alumni, section 2 was not, with four separate questionnaires being printed. As an example, the questionnaire mailed to all graduates majoring in retailing will be found in Resource B. This information is now being used in course and curriculum projects.

Other Sources. In collecting data, it is important to identify the specific "community" the program serves. In some instances it is the local area or a particular section of the state; in others, as in the survey of the Radio-Television Directors Association, it may be a national or international body of professionals. In the design of the previously mentioned teaching assistant orientation program, invaluable information was obtained at a national conference on teaching assistants sponsored by Ohio State University and from a national survey on teaching assistants by Diamond and Gray (1987). An informal survey of needs by the graduate student organization also proved most helpful. However, on both the curriculum and course levels, one must not overlook the portion of the college community that is closest at hand and thus easiest to ignore — the local community of faculty in related departments and in the department itself. If the course is a prerequisite to other courses, what do the faculty teaching these courses expect? Projects have failed because a significant group of faculty opposed the project for reasons often relatively unimportant; such failures could have been avoided if these faculty had been approached early in the design process. Overlooking these groups can be a particular problem in larger institutions in which departments within a single school or college may have developed a tendency to work independently or to compete with one another for both students and support dollars.

As mentioned earlier, we have also found that establishing an employer/alumni advisory committee for projects in professional schools has proved extremely beneficial both in the quality of their participation and in the resources they can bring to the project. An additional benefit has been the willingness of many committee members to open their companies to formal, cooperative internship programs.

Educational Priorities

Institutional priorities provide useful information and should be identified because a school, college, or university often has priorities that directly affect the design of a curriculum and of courses within it. These priorities are often shaped by dollar and material constraints that encourage focusing on one particular area or type of program and discourage focusing on another. They may determine the source and type of its students. Enrollment and dollar considerations, combined with the history of a given institution, all influence the programs that the institution offers and the students who enroll. A church-supported institution, for example, can be expected to have certain unique objectives. Likewise, we should not necessarily expect an institution located in a metropolitan area to have the same priorities or programs as one located in a rural setting. As needs differ, so should the characteristics and content of our academic programs.

It is also important to state clearly what the existing priorities are. If a principal aim of a lower-division course is to generate majors, this should be stated and understood. Unfortunately, this important objective is rarely admitted or discussed. There is nothing improper about trying to attract more students into a discipline, unless, of course, there is no need for such specialists and it is done solely to retain faculty positions. If this objective (attracting more students) is stated, greater emphasis can be placed on introducing the student to the discipline, the faculty, the department, the profession, and the program and on building a positive attitude toward them all.

Domain of Knowledge

Certainly the most obvious basic design input, the domain of knowledge has often been the chief, and sometimes only, consideration in curriculum and course change. Changes in knowledge do in time reach the classroom. However, these changes have been most obvious in disciplines in which governmental support has been available. Unfortunately, most significant modifications of course content have usually been of a "crash" nature to resolve discrepancies that became obvious enough to raise a national clamor for improvement. Content modification should be a continual process.

As discoveries are made, as theories are modified, and as

new areas evolve, the adjustment of the educational content should occur immediately. Therefore, on curriculum projects it is important that the instructional staff be selected to ensure that the content and scope of the program are as contemporary and academically sound as possible, and that a continual process for updating is included in the overall design. A review of major journals and of topics covered in national conferences along with conversations with professionals in the field are all excellent sources for identifying trends and content changes in the discipline. The music education department at Syracuse University used such sources in designing their curricular changes.

For example, to study the domain of music education, the faculty involved with the redesign of the curriculum undertook activities that included

1. Reading and studying music and music education books, especially those most current
2. Reading and analyzing articles, advertisements, and other information in the major professional journals in the discipline for the last ten years to identify general trends in the music education profession
3. Studying research related to the teaching of music by reviewing the literature for the past fifteen years
4. Reviewing and evaluating graduate research related to the teaching of music and reported in *Dissertation Abstracts* during the last fifteen years
5. Examining curriculum guidelines published by major professional groups
6. Surveying and studying the undergraduate music education programs of all colleges and universities in the state
7. Examining and analyzing the competency-based certification guidelines and recommendations made by the state education department
8. Reading and studying the literature written about competency-based teacher education, a national trend affecting teacher education programs in many states (Eickmann and Lee, 1976)

Research

While some overlap in data can be anticipated between this category and the others, there are, in any field, a number of studies being conducted that may be relevant to the project. These studies generally fall into three areas: the discipline as it relates to content, to future direction of the profession, and to pedagogy.

The Discipline — Content. In most professions, formal studies are being conducted to determine what content is appropriate for the field. In some instances, such as the work being done in industrial design, this may be sponsored by the national professional organization. In other instances, it may, as has been done with several of the Syracuse projects, be undertaken by a few faculty working independently on a course or curriculum project. Journals in the discipline that include articles on teaching and curriculum can often be an excellent source of information on recent studies related to course and program content. An additional reference is the *Journal of Higher Education* published by the Ohio State University Press and the American Association for Higher Education. For example, one issue reported research by Donald E. Powers and Mary K. Enright (1987) on analytical reasoning skills in graduate study that provides some useful data on the skills needed and the problems encountered by students in the fields of chemistry, computer science, education, engineering, English, and psychology, information that would be extremely useful to faculty developing a curriculum in any of these disciplines. Whatever the source, reviewing these studies can save significant time and effort or open up new paths of exploration.

The Discipline — Future Directions. The future direction of the profession or of the content/research component of the discipline should not be overlooked. Not only does reviewing the direction these areas may be taking ensure up-to-date content, but it also provides a foundation on which to base decisions regarding new content and objectives. Any new program, if it is to be successful, must be future oriented and based on the thinking of the outstanding practitioners and researchers in the field. A fine source for information on future trends in education is *Change* magazine, published by the Helen Dwight Reid Educational Foundation under the educational leadership of the American Association of Higher Education. For example, one issue (March/April 1986) focusing on improving the relationship between the liberal arts and technology included an article on "Learning to Think Like an Engineer: Why, What, and How." For faculty teaching in the other disciplines, the same issue includes a review of the Sloan Foundation's new liberal arts program, a description of ways in which technology is being introduced successfully into a number of liberal arts programs, and an article describing how science and nonscience faculty can work together to improve the teaching of science. The March/April 1988 issue of *Change* will particularly interest those involved in course and curriculum improvement; it contains an article on core curriculum and a report on factors related to high faculty morale in liberal arts colleges.

Pedagogy. Ongoing research examines how students think, how they learn, and how they can effectively be taught. While the findings about teaching and learning are most useful during the production and implementation stage, there are occasions when this information can significantly affect the overall structure of the program. For example, a decision to build on mastery learning or to use the Perry (1970) research on how the thinking of students changes with maturity could determine the structure of the course and the sequence of content. An excellent source of basic research in pedagogy as it applies to higher education is the federally sponsored National Center for Research to Improve Postsecondary Teaching and Learning at the University of Michigan. A useful publication is the ASHE *Handbook on Teaching and Instructional Resources,* edited by John J. Gardiner. The 1987 edition includes several comprehensive annotated bibliographies on higher education as a field of study and on teaching in postsecondary education.

Summary

The next step in the design of a course or curriculum focuses not on what is but what could be. Using data about students, the discipline, the community, and the institution, we design the "ideal" program. In this chapter we discussed the various questions that should be asked and the data that should be collected for use in the initial design phase. The quality of the data helps determine the success or failure of the project. To ensure that sufficient information is available for sound decision making, data should be collected in the following areas:

1. Students
   - entering level of competence
   - ability to meet assumed prerequisites
   - goals, priorities, and major
   - reasons for enrolling
   - attitudes about discipline, area, and so on
   - assumptions about course/program
2. Society (employers, recruiters, alumni, other faculty)
   - basic competencies all students should have upon graduation
   - field/discipline-specific requirements
   - existing gaps between what is needed and abilities of graduates
3. Educational priorities
   - mission of institution, program, department
   - general goals of the program (course)
4. Domain of knowledge
   - required/essential content
   - future trends in discipline/area of focus
   - accreditation requirements (professional programs, state)
   - new areas of content
5. Research
   - discipline-related
   - pedagogy (teaching and learning)

5

Developing a Design
for the Ideal
Course or Program

In this chapter, we will use several case studies to describe the initial design phase. These have been selected from a number of disciplines and address a wide range of academic problems. We also examine how data were used by some talented faculty and instructional support staff to solve some common instructional problems.

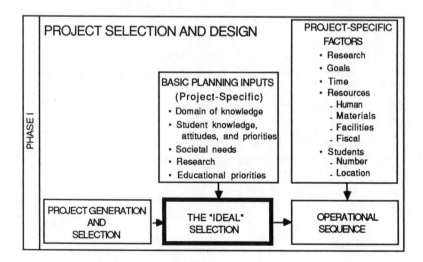

Overview

As actual designing begins on a course or curriculum, those involved use all the data that have been collected, their experiences, and their creativity to decide what an "ideal" program would look like. Since not all the data will be available immediately, one can anticipate that this will be a period of revision and a time of contemplation and discussion. Formal meetings are usually held no more than once a week, and bimonthly is not uncommon.

While fine tuning continues throughout the design and implementation process, few significant changes in sequence or content occur between the "ideal" conceptualization and what is actually offered. However, during the effort to reach for the ideal, the changes that take place in the design of a course or curriculum from one meeting to the next can be substantial. For example, Figures 5 and 6 are drafts 1 and 3 of the first semester of a two-semester course in Communications Design. Notice how the original idea of focusing on black and white line art in the first semester and color in the second was changed by the faculty member to an entirely different approach, with the number of color options available to the designer now serving as the focus of each unit. In addition, the laboratory portion of the course has begun, by the third draft, to take shape in both content and sequence. In some instances, major changes of this type evolve as the faculty continue to think about the course and answer questions posed by the instructional developer or other faculty. At other times changes result directly from comments of other faculty, professionals in the field, and so on, or may be based on additional data that have been collected. During this stage, modification is both facilitated and encouraged.

Dealing with a Lack of Prerequisites: Three Approaches

Case Study: Freshman English

There are few courses that generate as much emotion on any campus as the introductory course in writing. Disliked by

Figure 5. Communications Design: First Semester – Draft 1.

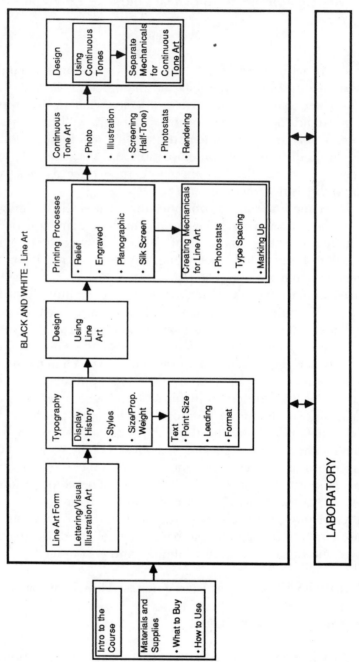

Source: Toni Toland, Robert M. Diamond.

Figure 6. Communications Design: First Semester – Draft 3.

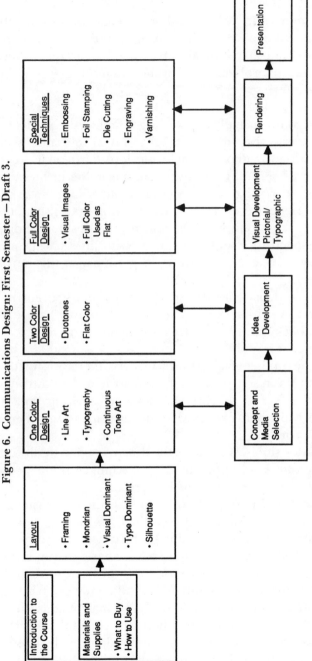

Source: Toni Toland, Robert M. Diamond.

most students and dealing with a subject that most faculty feel should have been taught (but was not) in the high schools, the freshman English (composition) course also presents a series of major design problems to anyone attempting to develop an effective offering.

1. The course usually enrolls large numbers of students and, to be effective, must be taught in relatively small sections.
2. Most English department faculty look down on the teaching of writing and, in addition, as specialists in literature or creative writing, often do not have the willingness, skills, or experience necessary to teach the subject. Consequently, on many large campuses the teaching of freshman English is delegated to graduate students with little background or interest in teaching writing or grammar at this particular level.
3. The students enter the program with an extremely wide range of writing skills. While a small number have an excellent background in writing, the majority do not.

The problem facing the faculty was, therefore, not unique: how, with the resources available, to structure an introductory course that would develop the necessary writing skills in all students while being sensitive to the extreme range of entering competencies.

A decision was made by the design team to totally rethink not only *what* was taught, but *how* it was taught. In the process, a number of major issues were addressed.

Content. In the past, the course, while emphasizing writing, used literature and poetry as the basis for the writing. The faculty concluded that a major problem with this approach is that it forced students who were having basic writing problems to write about subjects that were not only new to them but at times difficult to understand. As a result, it was often difficult to separate confusion about the subject from problems with structure and organization. They therefore concluded that if this course were to focus on writing, they would provide the students with the opportunity to write about subjects that were familiar to them until that time when they had developed basic skill in structuring and organizing their essays.

Structure and Time. Recognizing that students entered the course with a wide range of writing skills, the faculty explored a number of structural options for dealing with this diversity. Two related questions were raised by the instructional developer that were to have a significant impact on the design that was adopted. First, since students entered the course with such a wide range of writing skills, did they have to begin at the same place? And second, since students learn at different rates, was it necessary for all to take the same amount of time to reach an acceptable level of writing performance? When the decision was made that both beginning point and time could indeed be flexible, an entirely new approach to the design of the course became possible. As a result, the course that evolved not only allowed students to begin at different levels based on their entering competencies, but also permitted them to move through the course at their own pace.

Standardization Between Sections. Because the course relied heavily on teaching assistants, many of whom had little previous experience in the teaching of composition, it became obvious early in the design process that whatever structure evolved, it would have to facilitate standardization in grading. Not only would the criteria used for evaluating writing have to be taught to and understood by each of the teaching assistants and by the students, but grading standards would have to be consistent across all sections. To address this issue, a decision was made for the program to include a formal and required course in pedagogy for all new teaching assistants in which the grading protocol developed for this course is taught.

Evaluation and Placement. If students were to begin at different levels according to entry-level writing skills, the problem of assessment also had to be addressed. The faculty felt that existing tests could be used for this purpose and proposed a combination of a commercially produced diagnostic test with a written essay. After several years of use, the commercial test was replaced by one developed locally that was more suited to the specific needs of the course.

Remediation. One of the most difficult problems the faculty had to address was one of remediation—how to deal with those students who entered the course with writing problems at the basic level, having difficulty with punctuation, usage, agreement, and so on. While many faculty could and do claim that teaching of these skills is the responsibility of the primary and secondary schools, the fact remains that students enter college without these skills and they must be taught. The problem was even more complex since the vast majority of teaching assistants had little training or interest in teaching basic grammar and usage. The decision was made, therefore, to combine independent study using programmed texts with tutoring. Furthermore, this tutoring would be done not by the teaching assistant but by part-time instructors experienced in teaching basic writing and hired specifically for this purpose. An interesting sidelight is that the selection of the specific programmed sequences that were to be used turned out to be far more difficult than at first imagined. After identifying the specific skills they wished to have taught (approximately twenty), the faculty began a review of every programmed text on the market to identify those pages or frames that dealt effectively with specific topics. Although over thirty texts were available, the majority were found to be poorly written and to contain unacceptable treatment of some topics. In addition, one of the most effective publications was no longer available. After several years, a number of effective sequences were identified and used effectively. (At that time, there were no teaching machines or computer-based units that could be used for this purpose.)

Results. What evolved was a course that differed significantly in structure from the existing course and from most traditional programs. Basically, the course had the following characteristics (see Figure 7).

- Using data provided by two diagnostic tests (one objective, one essay), the faculty placed students in one of three instructional levels: I, basic skills; II, essay; and III, literature and independent writing.

Figure 7. Instructional Sequence: Freshman English.

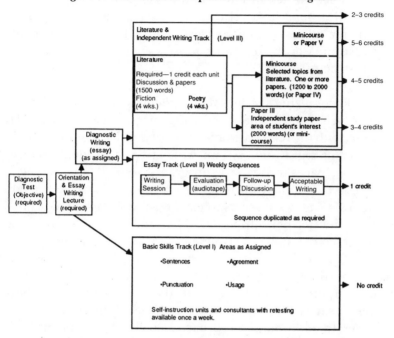

Note: Several changes in this format were made based on further field testing. Levels I and II were combined, with a greater emphasis being placed on individual counseling. In addition, the essay test replaced the objective instrument as the basis for placement.

On the basis of diagnostic tests, students are placed in one of three instructional levels. Level I students are assigned to specific remedial areas according to need; any may move up to Level II as soon as they can pass the criterion tests. Two passing papers are required before a student may move from Level II to Level III. In Level III students are required to take two four-week segments on Ficton and Poetry, and they may select from a series of minicourses or write a paper from an area of interest for additional credit. The required segments are repeated throughout the semester for the convenience of students moving into Level III during the year.

Source: Randall Brune, Robert M. Diamond.

- Students moved from level to level upon reaching specific and measurable levels of performance.
- Writing focused on subjects familiar to the student until Level III, when literature was first introduced.

- Class size varied by level with individual tutoring in Level I, small groups in Level II, and larger sections in Level III. (Later all levels limited class size to fifteen for teaching assistants and twenty for more experienced faculty and instructors.)

Recognizing the fact that students would move through the course at different speeds, the project team made early contact with the registrar's office. Out of this discussion evolved a continuous registration system, which permits students to move at various paces through the program—some taking as long as two years to complete the required six credits. The flexible credit system also allows students to earn from one to six credits in a single semester, permitting a modest number of better prepared students to complete the course in less than two semesters.

This design addresses remediation in Level I, the non-credit portion of the course. Research by Stern (1970) has shown that building remedial work into the regular program eliminates much of the stigma associated with "bonehead" English courses. In addition, the approach also eliminates the problem of awarding college credit for "noncollege" level work.

Case Study: Introductory Calculus

As traditionally taught, the basic sequence in calculus consisted of four sequential three-credit courses taken over the freshman and sophomore years. The sequence is required of all engineering, mathematics, economics, and science majors. Over the years, faculty teaching the course had become increasingly concerned with a high failure rate. In addition, studies had shown a direct and high correlation between achievement on the mathematics placement test taken by all entering freshmen and success in the traditional course. In other words, those students who entered with a solid mathematics background tended to pass; all others did not.

To address these issues, a self-paced program that was based on the mastery concept of learning was developed and introduced. This program used the continuous registration and flexible credit systems implemented earlier for use in other courses. Students enrolled in the initial field-testing version of the course slightly over four months after design work began. This rapid design and implementation sequence was made possible by the fact that the content and the sequence materials presented were traditional (not open to significant review) and that the course was built around an available commercial text. Student guides, manuals, and some instructional materials, however, were developed specifically for the new program to permit its implementation.

The goal of self-paced calculus is to permit students to master the materials covered in an introductory college calculus course at a pace most comfortable to them. The subject matter is divided into units (or blocks of material) that typically take about one week to cover and learn thoroughly. The students use a standard calculus textbook and a set of detailed study guides to learn the material in each unit. Regularly scheduled tutorial periods are also available. Problem-solving sessions are provided on an optional basis, and two programmed booklets were written to teach content not covered adequately or effectively in the available materials. A page from the student manual describing the course is found in Figure 8.

For each unit a series of parallel tests was prepared. When the students believe that they have mastered the material in a unit, they may request a test for that particular unit. A student who passes at a prespecified level of mastery may begin to prepare for the next unit. Students who do not pass are given tutorial help or remedial assignments and must then take another version of the test for that same unit. Again, a pass is required before proceeding to the next unit. Unit tests may be taken as often as needed with no grade penalty for not passing. Tests for all units are available from the beginning of the course so that any student who has prior preparation in calculus may receive credit by passing the appropriate unit tests.

In order to earn one academic credit, the students must pass four units successfully; eight units passed earns two credits, twelve units passed earns three credits, and so on. Thus, the speed at which the students progress through the course and the number of credits individuals earn depends on how rapidly they can master the material. A separate letter grade is earned and recorded for each credit hour.

A follow-up study of 248 students, 60 in the self-paced program and 188 from the conventional offering, showed the primary goals have been reached. First, the correlation between entry-level test results and performance in the course has been

Figure 8. Self-Paced Calculus Course Sequence.

- TESTS FOR ALL UNITS WILL BE AVAILABLE DURING THE TUTORIAL PERIODS AND MAY BE TAKEN WHEN YOU BECOME PREPARED FOR THEM.

- FAILED UNIT TESTS MAY BE RETAKEN UNTIL PASSED, WITH NO PENALTY.

- SATISFACTORY COMPLETION OF EACH UNIT TEST IS REQUIRED BEFORE PROCEEDING TO THE NEXT TEST.

- THERE IS NO LIMIT TO THE NUMBER OF CREDITS THAT YOU MAY EARN IN ANY SEMESTER.

MATH 295, 296, UNITS 1–24 (4 UNIT TESTS = 1 CREDIT)

4-CREDIT PACE: COMPLETION OF 16 UNITS PER SEMESTER

3-CREDIT PACE: COMPLETION OF 12 UNITS PER SEMESTER

2-CREDIT PACE: 8 UNITS PER SEMESTER

MATH 397, 398 UNITS 25–42 (3 UNIT TESTS = 1 CREDIT)

4-CREDIT PACE: COMPLETION OF 12 UNITS PER SEMESTER

3-CREDIT PACE: COMPLETION OF 9 UNITS PER SEMESTER

2-CREDIT PACE: 6 UNITS PER SEMESTER

Figure 9. Mathematics Preparation × Instructional Method Interaction.

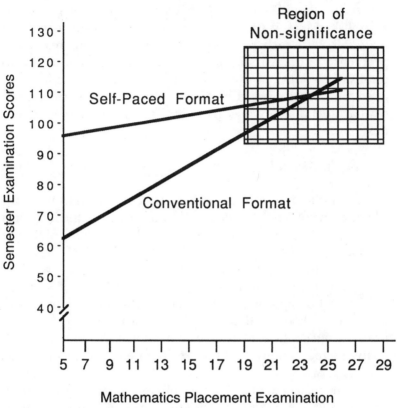

Source: Pascarella, 1977.

significantly reduced. In the conventional course, math place-ment exam results had a direct relationship to semester exam-ination scores, whereas in the self-paced course, this rela-tionship was substantially reduced as entry-level problems were dealt with and corrected (see Figure 9).

Secondly, there has also been a major improvement in overall student performance. As with any self-paced course, it was necessary to build into the course or program a minimum pace—a rate of movement below which students could not fall. While there was no maximum limit, students are required to complete eight units in their first semester—a two-credit-per-semester pace. One caution about materials arises from this course and should be mentioned. Relying, as the course does, on a published text, it was necessary to rewrite all the associated materials with each revision of the text. This has become a problem over the years as the publisher of the text has tended to publish new editions every two or three years. To reduce the need for extensive rewriting of associated materials, the university has stockpiled extra copies of the text from one year to the next.

Case Study: General Chemistry

Another interesting and successful project in which time, rather than content, was the significant variable is the introductory general chemistry course offered at the University of Rhode Island.

The problem was not unusual: a high failure rate (30 percent) and a related frustration level on the part of both the faculty and many students. With an analysis of student profile data, faculty learned that the majority of those who failed or dropped out could be identified even before the course began by analyzing their entering SAT scores, high school class rank, and math ability.

The instructor, Jacklyn Vitlimberger, proposed an experiment that was implemented with the approval of her chairman during the 1985–1986 academic year. In this project, a number of "high-risk" students were enrolled in a new two-semester general chemistry course that had the *identical* content, assignments, instructional objectives, and instructor as the existing one-semester program. The additional time was used to provide the students with an increased opportunity to practice the problem-solving skills that were identified as required for success in general chemistry. The examinations in both courses were also identical; the midterm in the traditional program became the first-semester final examination in the experimental two-semester program, and both sections took the same final comprehensive examination. The performance of students in the two-semester program was then compared with that of students in the one-semester program who had the same range of SAT scores, class rank, and math test scores.

Results. The results were extremely positive.

- Seventy percent of the "high-risk" students in the two-semester program passed the course and the final examination.
- *Each* of the students in the experimental section who completed the two-semester sequence scored *above* the median score of the students in the traditional sections on the final examination.
- The overall failure rate in the course was significantly reduced (from 30 percent to approximately 10 percent).
- High-risk students who completed the two-semester sequence also performed satisfactorily in subsequent science and math courses.

As a result of this project, the experimental two-semester course was regularized, and entering students who are identified as being in the high-risk category are encouraged to enroll in this option.

A Question of Academic Credit. In its experimental format, students received no credit for the first semester and three credits for the second. This approach placed a hardship on a number of students who were in the experimental section. Since they required twelve credits of course work to maintain full-time academic standing for purposes of financial support, "work study," and so on, they were forced to enroll in five courses the first semester rather than four because the chemistry course carried no credit. Enrolling in five courses a semester was too heavy an academic load for such high-risk students. These issues were resolved by granting three credits for each semester of the revised course but with the stipulation that only the second semester credits count toward a degree. Grades for the first semester are, however, included in the student's grade point average (GPA). Awarding credit in this manner allows an institution to meet the needs of academically disadvantaged students *without* lowering the academic standards of the course, the department, or the institution.

Case Study: Introductory Economics

In many instances the entry-level deficiencies in mathematics noted above are due to students' avoidance of the subject rather than to neglect of these skills (multiplication, division, fractions, decimals, and percents, solving word problems, and the use of graphs) in the final three or four years of precollege education.

Economics, like many of the social sciences, relies heavily on mathematics for the presentation and interpretation of data. It was therefore not surprising to find in a project that included the redesign of the two existing introductory courses, microeconomics and macroeconomics, and the introduction of a new course designed specifically for the noneconomics major that the issue of mathematics prerequisites would have to be addressed.

As a first step, a review was made of the text that would be used and of past examinations to identify which specific mathematics competencies would be required of the students. Identified competencies were the basic use of fractions, decimals, and percents and a heavy reliance on the use of tables and graphic analyses to represent the relationship between economic variables.

Before major design work began, a basic mathematics skill assessment test was constructed around these prerequisite elements and administered on the second day of class to a group of students enrolled in the basic microeconomics course that was then being offered. This testing not only provided data on the mathematics skills of the students enrolled in the course, but permitted items on the test itself to be evaluated. Data collected showed that the concern of the faculty was legitimate: nearly 70 percent of the students had inadequate mathematics skills in at least one area. As a result, a diagnostic and remedial sequence (see Figure 10) was built into the structure of all three introductory courses since all enrolled first-time economics students.

Figure 10. Beginning Sequence—Economics 201.

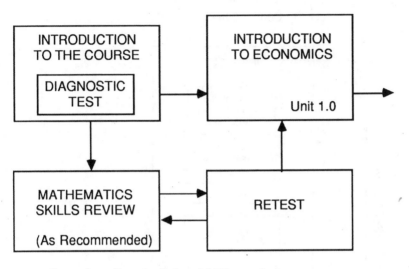

Source: Jerry Evensky, Robert M. Diamond.

A decision was made to use a diagnosic test followed by remedial programmed units that would be assigned on the basis of test results. Although students were actively encouraged to complete the sequence, the units were not required. Students are, however, provided with their test results and an analysis of the relationship of test results to performance in the course. An exhaustive search of available programmed and computer materials failed to locate appropriate materials for use in economics. For this reason, programmed units were designed specifically to meet this need, with work under way to develop computer-aided instruction. In addressing problems of this type, it is also possible to build the remediation into the formal instruction while exempting those students who have the competency from the class session. This option was not taken in this instance since designers agreed that the problem could be effectively eliminated for most students by five hours of out-of-class study and that using in-class time for this purpose would be wasteful.

It has now become possible to advise some students, on

Figure 11. Introduction to the Study of Religion.

Course Overview

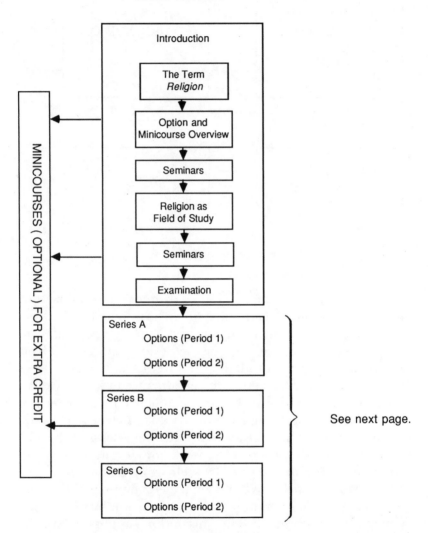

Note: This course in religion provides students with a variety of required options and an opportunity to earn extra credit by taking additional options or minicourses. Classes are scheduled for two hours, twice weekly, with a different series of options offered each hour—permitting a student to complete two option credits in any four-week period.

Source: Ronald Cavanagh, Robert M. Diamond.

the basis of extensive data, to either complete these sequences or, in severe cases, take additional mathematics courses if they hope to succeed in economics.

Dealing with Student Diversity

Case Study: Introduction to the Study of Religion

Earlier we discussed the data collected during this project, describing the interest levels and understanding that students brought to their first course in religion. The data showed an extremely wide diversity in backgrounds and interest levels. The structure developed was based on this information and

Figure 11. Introduction to the Study of Religion (continued).

OPTIONS		
Three options are required, one from each area. Each additional option is worth one additional credit.		
Forms of Religious Expression	Forms of Religious Issues	Methodologies
Myth	Paths of Salvation	Historical
Belief	Death and Eschatology	Psychological
Ritual		Philosophical
Sacred Text	Evil and Suffering	Comparative/ Structural
Community Structure	Sacred and Secular	Sociological
	God and Reason	
	Religious Experience of the Oppressed	

other priorities of the department. Several key operating goals for the course evolved.

- A common framework for the course and appropriate vocabulary had to be set.
- The course had to relate to major interest areas of the students.
- Since the course is the initial contact the students have with the department, it had to serve as a recruiting vehicle for majors and for enrollments in other courses.

The unique course design that was developed proved most effective in meeting each of these objectives. Seminars and programmed materials were used to introduce the term *religion* and religion as a field of study (see Figure 11, pp. 82–83). From this point, students were required to take one four-week option from each of three major areas: Forms of Religious Expression, Forms of Religious Issues, and Methodologies. Additional options could be taken for extra credit. An advantage of this design (referred to by some as the "Chinese menu" approach) was that it allowed freshmen to have direct contact in small group sessions with senior religion faculty teaching in their areas of specialization. Options with higher enrollments were repeated as needed.

An interesting sidelight is that when the new course was first taught, a small number of students in the class felt strongly that religion as a formal subject did not belong in a university. For this reason, an optional unit, "Objections to the Study of Religion," was built into the program. As the political climate of the country changed during the 1970s, the number of students enrolling in this option declined significantly, and the option was dropped.

Case Study: Cost Effectiveness

This graduate course, offered by the School of Education, forced the faculty member teaching it to face two important problems.

- How to meet the needs of an extremely diverse student population: majors in higher education, management, and instructional technology, many of whom were from a number of different countries
- How to deal with some entering students who did not have a number of prerequisites

As part of the enrollment procedure that was developed, students are asked to complete a brief questionnaire that provides information for the instructor about why they are enrolling, related courses and work experiences they have had, and what their future professional goals are. This information is then used by the instructor to prepare assignments and identify student teams for projects later in the course (see Figure 12). What is particularly significant in this design is how students are allowed to focus on their own area of interest while applying the general model that is being taught. This occurs in two areas: Unit 4.0, in which the students apply the model to case studies, and Unit 5.0, for class projects. While it is not shown in this diagram, which covers only the second part of the course, at the beginning of the course students are given additional background reading and other assignments if their background in evaluation is inadequate.

This course represents an excellent example of how the basic content of a course can be left unchanged while the course itself is restructured to meet the specific needs of the students who are enrolled.

Dealing with a Curriculum

Up to this point, our major focus has been at the course level, but the same general process is followed when dealing with an entire curriculum. Here, however, the focus is on developing the relationship among the major instructional elements of a program. In time, these elements become individual courses or sequences of courses. In working at the curriculum level, unless the curriculum is entirely new, usually some existing courses remain as they are, others are modified (changes in content,

Figure 12. Cost Effectiveness in Instruction and Training.

COURSE DESCRIPTION

Part II

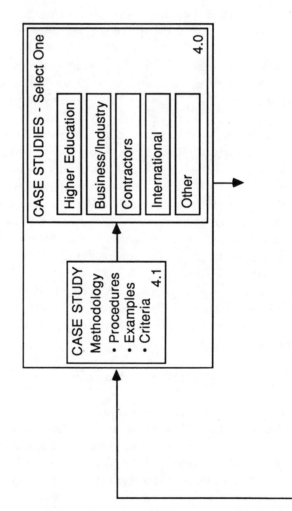

CASE STUDY

Methodology
• Procedures
• Examples
• Criteria   4.1

CASE STUDIES - Select One

Higher Education

Business/Industry

Contractors

International

Other

4.0

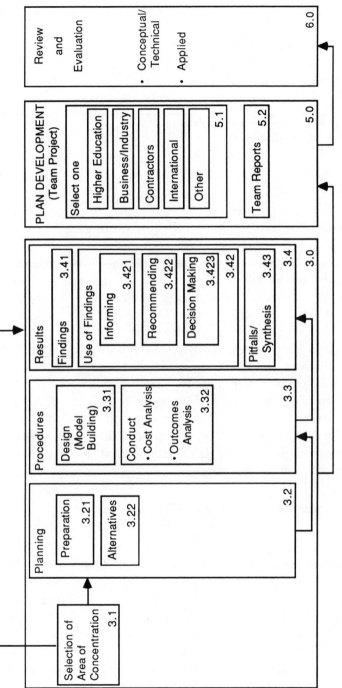

Source: Philip Doughty.

sequences, or credit hours), while still others are eliminated as new courses are introduced. As will be described in more detail in the next chapter, the new or revised courses are then designed from the beginning using this same model.

Case Study: Bachelor of Music/Music Industry

Figure 13 (pp. 90–91) represents the lower-division structure of a new curriculum, Music/Music Industry. Notice in particular the features that create individualized sequential movement: (1) attention has been paid to general entrance requirements and then to the program itself, (2) in the first two years only one new course is added—Music Industry, and (3) those students who enter with competency in two instruments have the option of taking a special three-course sequence in the School of Management. Discussions with professionals in the field, an extensive review of the literature, and numerous surveys were used to provide the data upon which both the curriculum and course designs were based.

The faculty thought that adding this overview course was essential as it would not only introduce the students to the field, but provide them with an understanding of the profession before they were required, at the end of their sophomore year, to select a major field of specialization and to apply for formal admission into the program.

Case Study: Master's Degree in Management

Figures 14 (p. 92) and 15 (pp. 94–95) are the beginning parts of two drafts of a proposed master's in business administration (MBA) program in management. A complex curriculum involving several departments, this project took many months to complete. Notice that while some elements in the sixth draft appear to have undergone little change, by the fourteenth version the structure itself has not only changed but has become far more specific. Major emphasis during this period was on two issues: first, what topics should be required of all students, and second, in what order. In addition, the fact that many MBA students enter with work experience had to be addressed.

This project did not begin until all departments in the school agreed to actively participate—a process that took nearly one year. By the time the project was completed, eighteen months later, it included a general description of the total curriculum with a list of student performance outcomes for each course or unit within it.

The design that evolved had several significant structural elements. Notice first how sensitive this structure was to the entry level of the students. While some students enroll directly from an undergraduate program that may or may not be in the field, others are older students entering after a number of years of work experience. Individual counseling and formal evaluation permit the assigning of prerequisite courses as they are needed. The Managerial Team Dynamics and Leadership Development sequence was added specifically to develop the "survival skills" (speech, interpersonal, and writing skills, and so on) that were highlighted again and again by employers and recruiters as being essential for success in the field. Notice also that in the Instructional Core (3.0), although some units (or courses) are required of all students, others are assigned according to the student's specific major on the basis of decisions made by each academic area. Also notice that career counseling and place-ment are not left to chance but have been proposed as an integral part of the total curriculum, and notice how the use of the terms (as required) in Unit 1.5 and (as assigned) in Unit 3.4 significantly simplify the diagraming process.

Although resource limitation restricted the full imple-mentation of the "idealized" curriculum, many elements are, in fact, being offered.

Case Study: Instructional Design, Development, and Evaluation

This graduate department, within the School of Educa-tion at Syracuse University, serves an extremely diverse student population that includes a number of international students, students who are returning to higher education after a number

Figure 13. Bachelor of Music/Music Industry Curriculum.

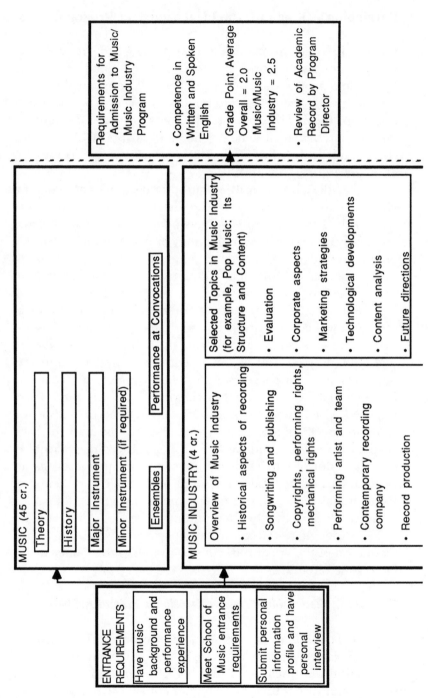

ENTRANCE REQUIREMENTS

Have music background and performance experience

Meet School of Music entrance requirements

Submit personal information profile and have personal interview

MUSIC (45 cr.)

Theory

History

Major Instrument

Minor Instrument (if required)

Ensembles   Performance at Convocations

MUSIC INDUSTRY (4 cr.)

Overview of Music Industry

• Historical aspects of recording

• Songwriting and publishing

• Copyrights, performing rights, mechanical rights

• Performing artist and team

• Contemporary recording company

• Record production

Selected Topics in Music Industry (for example, Pop Music: Its Structure and Content)

• Evaluation

• Corporate aspects

• Marketing strategies

• Technological developments

• Content analysis

• Future directions

Requirements for Admission to Music/Music Industry Program

• Competence in Written and Spoken English

• Grade Point Average Overall = 2.0 Music/Music Industry = 2.5

• Review of Academic Record by Program Director

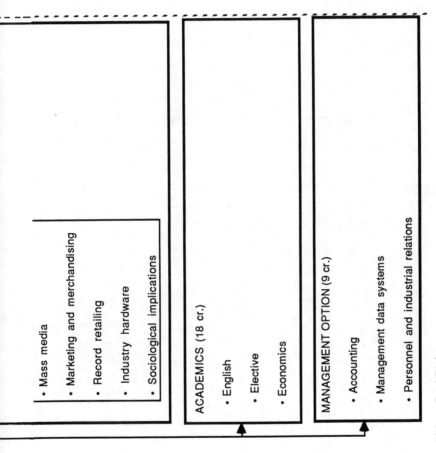

- Mass media
- Marketing and merchandising
- Record retailing
- Industry hardware
- Sociological implications

ACADEMICS (18 cr.)

- English
- Elective
- Economics

MANAGEMENT OPTION (9 cr.)

- Accounting
- Management data systems
- Personnel and industrial relations

Source: Ronald Lee, Paul Eickmann.

Figure 14. School of Management Proposed Master's Degree Program – Draft 6.

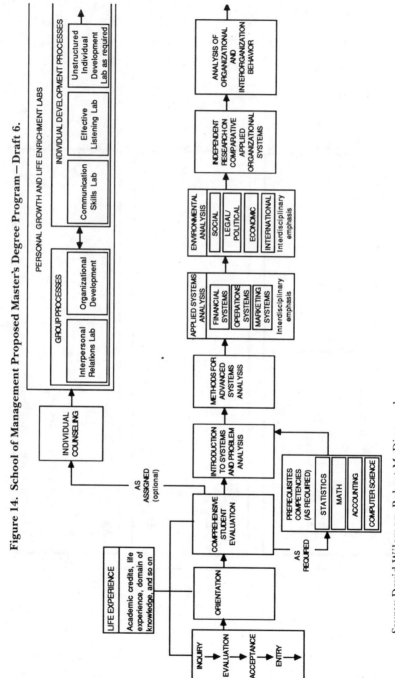

Source: David Wilemon, Robert M. Diamond.

of years in business, industry, and education, and some who are entering the field directly after completing undergraduate degrees. In addition, the program that was to be developed needed to serve the needs of both full- and part-time students. While the faculty wished to rethink both their master's and doctoral programs, a decision was made to focus first on the master's degree since many of the elements of this program would become prerequisites for the more advanced degree. The small department of six faculty members decided not to begin work on the curriculum until everyone could participate, and as a result, plans were made to begin the project during the summer. By September, the design was ready for presentation to students and other faculty in the school.

To assist in the design process, a survey was developed and administered to alumni. A special insert for recent graduates and present students focused on the present program (see Exhibit 2, pp. 96–97). Whereas the basic instrument included questions on the importance of major program areas, on practical experiences that contributed to their education, and on their ratings of the importance of a number of professional and personal traits, the insert focused on advisement, admission procedures, placement, and assessment.

As faculty reviewed the data and discussed their own concerns about the existing program, several key issues evolved. These ranged from the need to provide exemption from certain elements of the program for those students who entered with related on-the-job experiences to the desire to develop a program that provided all students with basic discipline-related competencies in a manner that was both sequential and logical. For these reasons, the major focus of the initial effort was on the design of the core program, identifying what would be in it, in what order elements would be offered, and how it would relate to the areas of specialization that were necessary.

The sequence that developed was interesting in a number of ways (Figure 16, pp. 98–99).

• A weekend retreat would be used to introduce the program, the major elements within it (development and evaluation),

Figure 15. School of Management Proposed Master's Degree Program—Draft 14.

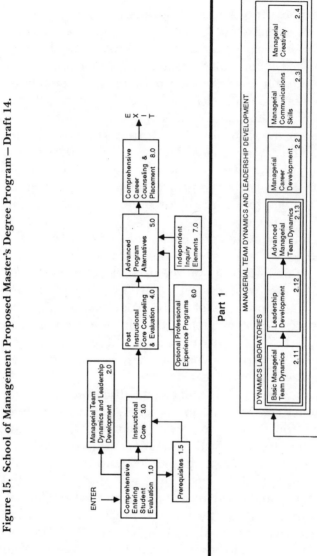

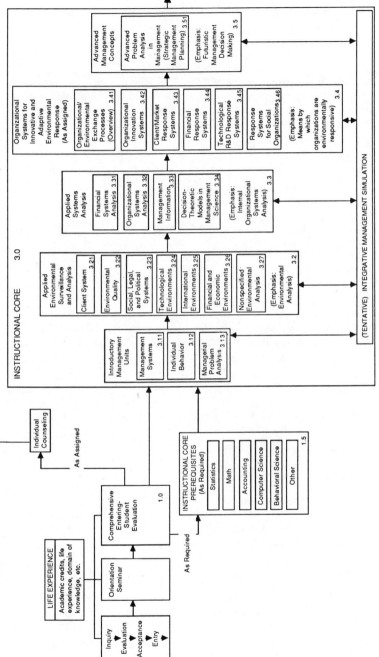

Source: David Wilemon, Robert M. Diamond.

Exhibit 2. Questionnaire Insert for Recent Graduates.

Instructional Design, Development, and Evaluation (IDD&E)
Recent Graduates Insert — Program Elements

A. How would you rate the *advisement* you received during your IDD&E
   program? (Circle the appropriate response and comment; give examples of effective and ineffective procedures.)   *(1–4)*

	Very Poor	Poor	Fair	Good	Very Good
1. Academic (courses, program)	1	2	3	4	5 *(5)*
comments and examples:					*(6–8)*
2. Career (internships, jobs)	1	2	3	4	5 *(9)*
comments and examples:					*(10–12)*
3. Dissertation	1	2	3	4	5 *(13)*
comments and examples:					*(14–16)*

B. 1. How would you rate the *admissions procedures* (including communica-
      tions) at IDD&E? (Circle the appropriate response)

Very Poor	Poor	Fair	Good	Very Good
1	2	3	4	5

   (17)

   2. Suggestions for improvement: *(18–20)*

C. 1. How would you rate the *orientation* you received upon entering the
      IDD&E program? (Circle the appropriate response)

Very Poor	Poor	Fair	Good	Very Good
1	2	3	4	5

   (21)

   2. Suggestions for improvement: *(22–24)*

D. 1. How would you rate the *placement assistance* offered by IDD&E?
      (Circle the appropriate response)

Very Poor	Poor	Fair	Good	Very Good
1	2	3	4	5

   (25)

   2. Suggestions for improvement: *(26–28)*

E. 1. Please rate the effectiveness of the following assessment and
      appraisal methods used in IDD&E. (VI = Very Ineffective, N =
      Neutral, VE = Very Effective, NA = Not Applicable; Circle the appro-
      priate response.)

	VI		N		VE	NA	
a. Master's comprehensives/intensives	1	2	3	4	5	NA	*(29)*
b. Portfolio (doctoral preliminary)	1	2	3	4	5	NA	
c. Doctoral qualifying exams	1	2	3	4	5	NA	
d. Dissertation proposal defense	1	2	3	4	5	NA	
e. Dissertation defense	1	2	3	4	5	NA	*(33)*

   2. Please make any comments or suggestions on how we may improve
      assessment and appraisal methods at IDD&E.   *(34–37)*

F. 1. How would you rate the general quality of the IDD&E program in terms of: (VP = Very Poor, P = Poor, F = Fair, G = Good, VG = Very Good; Circle the appropriate response)

	VP	P	F	G	VG	
a. Intellectual stimulation	1	2	3	4	5	*(38)*
b. Academic/Intellectual freedom	1	2	3	4	5	
c. Collegiality with faculty	1	2	3	4	5	
d. Friendliness of support staff	1	2	3	4	5	
e. Camaraderie with other graduate students	1	2	3	4	5	
f. Opportunity to explore outside interests	1	2	3	4	5	*(43)*

2. Please make any comments or suggestions on how we may improve the general quality of the IDD&E program.   *(44–47)*

Thank you for your assistance!

---

and the specific process or model upon which both would be based. It would also serve as an opportunity for the new students to meet the faculty and each other in a somewhat informal setting (A).

- One course, Learning Theory, would be taken before all others and serve as a base for what would follow (B).
- A number of basic skills would be developed within the core courses (C), and students having deficiencies in these areas would, at the conclusion of the introductory course, be required to take skill-building courses to improve these skills. In addition, the inclusion of these skills in the core courses would not be left to chance. Specific skills would be assigned for use on a course-by-course basis; that is, students would be required to use computers in certain courses and make formal presentations in others, and so on.
- The basic development model would be reinforced throughout the program by the use of case studies with the appropriate areas of learning theory and evaluation built into these same exercises (D).
- Running concurrently with the development core for full-time students and available sequentially for part-time students would be courses providing an overview of the field (E) and of instructional evaluation (F).

Several other courses are offered later in the core but are not shown in this figure. In addition, tracks of specialization

Figure 16. Proposed Master's Degree in Instructional Design, Development, and Evaluation.

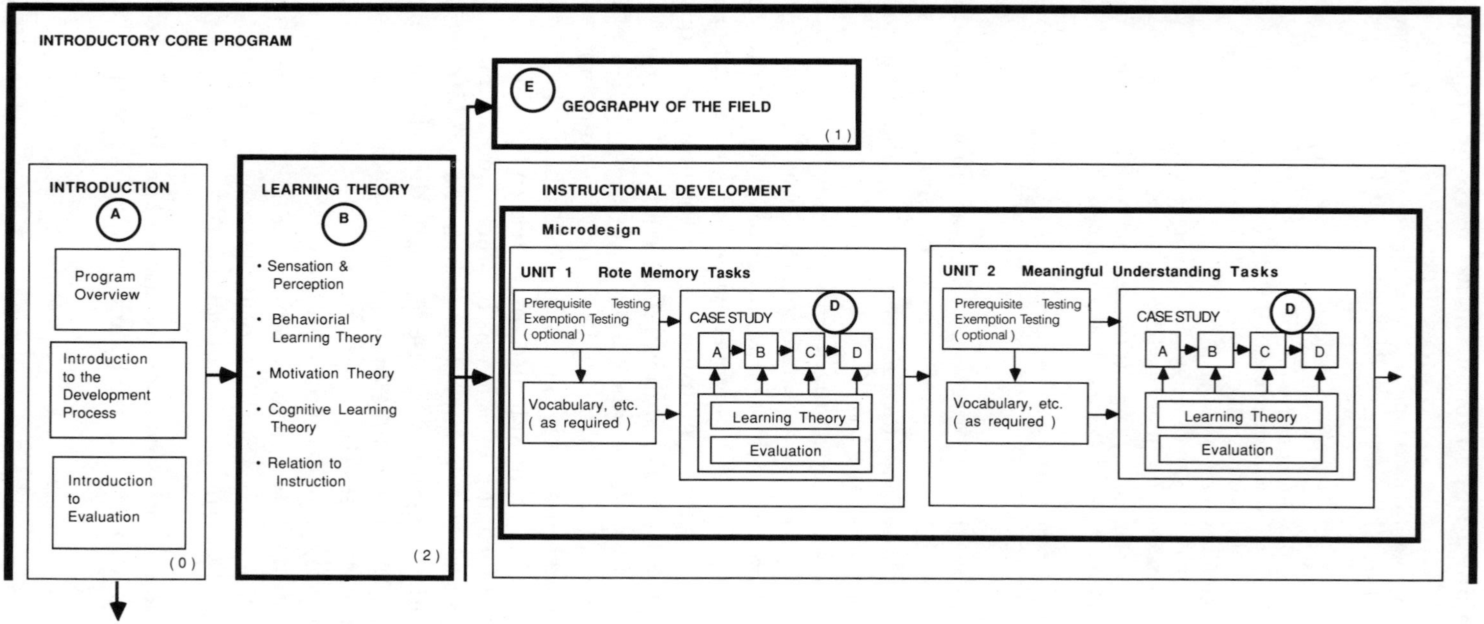

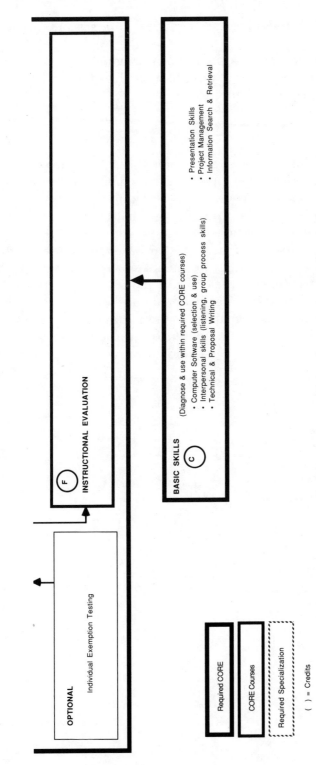

OPTIONAL

Individual Exemption Testing

F INSTRUCTIONAL EVALUATION

BASIC SKILLS

C (Diagnose & use within required CORE courses)

· Computer Software (selection & use)
· Interpersonal skills (listening, group process skills)
· Technical & Proposal Writing

· Presentation Skills
· Project Management
· Information Search & Retrieval

Required CORE

CORE Courses

Required Specialization

( ) = Credits

Source: Donald Ely, Philip Doughty, Barbara Grabowski, Charles Reigeluth, Alexander Romiszowski, Nick Smith.

were developed, and a preliminary assignment of credits was completed by the end of this phase, as shown in the lower left-hand corner of the figure.

Summary

In this chapter, we have discussed designing an ideal program. We have attempted, by using a number of examples, to illustrate how each course or curriculum is unique. There is simply no single all-purpose design that fits all cases. As students, faculty, institutions, resources, and disciplines vary, so must the course or curriculum that is developed. Notice that, although we have discussed content and structure, we have, for the most part, spent little effort in exploring instructional formats or in developing instructional objectives. These activities take place much later in the process. In the next chapter, we will describe how this idealized version, through analysis of resources, options, field tests, and so on, is modified into the program that is offered.

6

Adjusting
the Ideal
to the Real

In this chapter, we move from the ideal to the operational design. After a discussion on how course and curriculum projects differ, the chapter describes the various factors that determine how close the actual program that is offered will be to the ideal. Case studies are included.

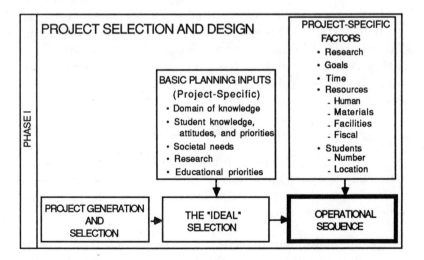

Overview

At some point in the development process, the preliminary or "ideal" instructional design phase is completed, and modifications begin to meet the practical limitations of the real world. This transition from the "ideal" to the "real" is gradual and, in reality, it is impossible to identify the point at which one stage ends and another begins. The separation is described here more for clarity of presentation than for representation of the actual process.

There are, however, as noted previously, fundamental differences from this point on between curriculum projects and those focusing on a single course. These are differences in detail, in purpose, and in the factors that must be considered. In addition, while curriculum projects terminate at the completion of this phase, course-related projects move on into the production, implementation, and evaluation activities of Phase II. See Figure 17.

At some point in a curriculum design, the focus shifts from the total curriculum to the courses within it. This change occurs once the operational diagram is complete and it becomes possible to identify courses that need major revision and new courses that must be developed. For these courses, the design process begins again with the project now focusing on individual courses that will become part of the new curriculum. The materials produced at the completion of this phase have also served effectively as the supporting documentation required by school, college, or institution curriculum committees responsible for approval of new programs or new courses.

Curriculum Projects: Factors to Consider

In moving from the "ideal" to the "real," or operational curriculum, several major factors must be taken into consideration — factors that are, in some instances, controlled by forces outside the department. These factors include

- Accreditation requirements: Does the proposed curriculum include those academic areas, credits, and courses required

Figure 17. The Development Process—Curriculum and Course Projects:
A Comparison.

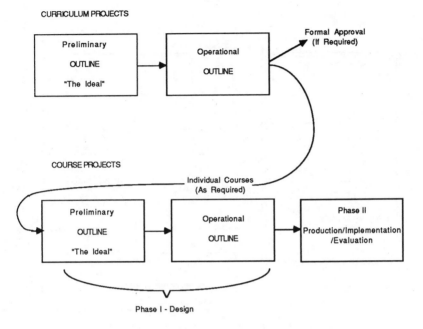

CURRICULUM PROJECTS

COURSE PROJECTS

Phase I - Design

by the institution or by external professional associations?
These may range from a basic liberal arts core to mandated
specialized technical or professional courses.

- Credit restrictions: Can the proposed program fit within the
  number of credit hours required for the degree involved?
  State departments of education, individual institutions,
  schools or colleges, and often external certification agencies place a minimum and a maximum on the number of
  credits a student may be required to take within and outside
  a single academic area or discipline. Are these standards
  being met?
- Fiscal and staff constraints: Is the proposed curriculum
  feasible? Can it be staffed? If new positions and new facilities
  are required, can the needed fiscal resources be found? For
  example, if class size is to be reduced to permit oral presentations or group projects, can the course be staffed?

Figure 18. The Retailing Major: Proposed Curriculum—Draft 3.

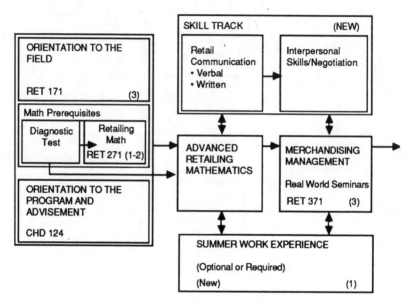

Source: Albert J. Harris, Robert M. Diamond.

- Effectiveness of existing courses and programs: If some elements of an existing curriculum are to be used, are they effective and do they meet the needs for which they have been selected?

It is important to stress that the process of answering some of these questions must involve the dean of the school or college and, in some instances, the academic vice-president as well. Therefore, involving these individuals with the project from the beginning is essential. While their active participation is not necessary, they must have early knowledge of what is being proposed and why.

Changes in structure are quite likely to occur as the curriculum moves from the ideal to what realistically can be offered.

Years 3 and 4

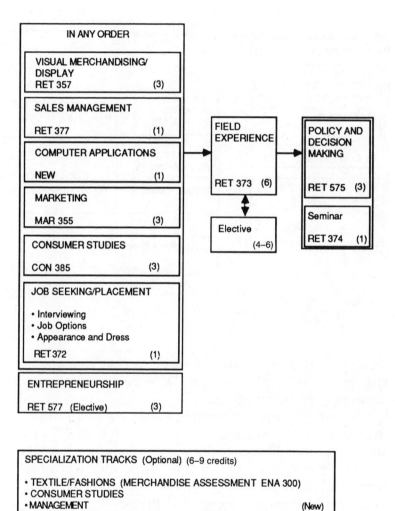

Figure 18 is the third draft of the idealized version of an undergraduate curriculum in retailing. Figure 19 is the operational version of the same program. While the general content stayed the same, over the ten-month period between these two

Figure 19. The Retailing Major: Proposed Curriculum — Draft 4.

Year 1   Year 2

Source: Albert J. Harris, Robert M. Diamond.

versions there were, as can be seen in the diagrams, significant changes in the overall sequences. These modifications were the result of three major factors.

First, an analysis of existing faculty resources and of the total number of credits that could be required during a single semester or over the total four years of the program showed that several of the original ideas would not be possible as planned. As a result, the proposed one-credit basic skills track (communications, and so on) was combined with the existing one-credit Job Seeking and Placement course into a three-credit course that students are required to take prior to their field experience. In addition, the new computer applications unit, rather than standing alone as an upper-division requirement, was moved into the three-credit Advanced Retailing Mathematics course.

The second major factor was the effectiveness of some of

Years 3 and 4

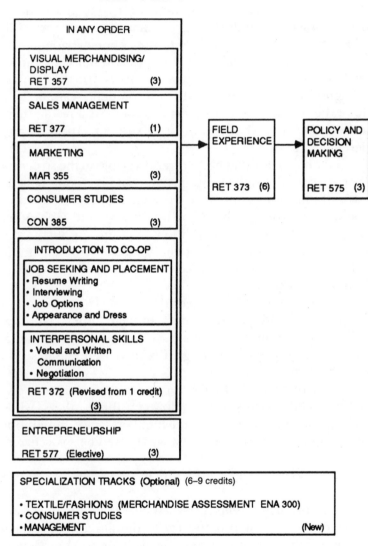

IN ANY ORDER

VISUAL MERCHANDISING/
DISPLAY
RET 357 (3)

SALES MANAGEMENT

RET 377 (1)

MARKETING

MAR 355 (3)

CONSUMER STUDIES

CON 385 (3)

INTRODUCTION TO CO-OP

JOB SEEKING AND PLACEMENT
• Resume Writing
• Interviewing
• Job Options
• Appearance and Dress

INTERPERSONAL SKILLS
• Verbal and Written
  Communication
• Negotiation

RET 372 (Revised from 1 credit)
(3)

ENTREPRENEURSHIP

RET 577 (Elective) (3)

FIELD
EXPERIENCE

RET 373 (6)

POLICY AND
DECISION
MAKING

RET 575 (3)

SPECIALIZATION TRACKS (Optional) (6–9 credits)

• TEXTILE/FASHIONS (MERCHANDISE ASSESSMENT ENA 300)
• CONSUMER STUDIES
• MANAGEMENT (New)

INTERNATIONAL FASHION
RETAILING
(In London) (Optional)

RET 400 (New) (3)

the courses. Data showed that the single retailing mathematics course was not successful. Passing the math prerequisite test, while encouraged, was not required. Consequently, students who had worked diligently throughout their academic careers to avoid mathematics entered this important course inadequately prepared. In the revised program, a basic math skills laboratory was added and is now required of all students who do not pass the diagnostic mathematics skills test. Students cannot continue in the program until this test is passed. As a result, there have been positive changes in both student attitudes and achievement.

The final factor that had a direct bearing on the structure of the curriculum was the support that could be found outside the department for cooperative programs. Specialized tracks are being developed both within the college and with other schools of the university. In addition, with the support of the university's Division of International Programs Abroad, an optional fashion/retailing course at a London site is now being offered by the department.

Clearly, information collected from recruiters, employers, and alumni had a direct impact on the computer applications unit, the communications area, and the interpersonal skills area and supported strongly the increased emphasis on basic mathematics.

Interestingly, in the final version of this program only one of the required courses is new. However, three others, while retaining their course names and numbers, have undergone major revisions. In two of these, changes in credit also occurred.

Course Projects: Factors to Consider

As mentioned previously, when curriculum projects are completed, the next step is to turn to designing in the ideal those courses that are either new or need major revision. Course projects, on the other hand, now move from the "ideal" to an operational design so that at the end of this phase the process of production, implementation, evaluation, and revision can begin. Experience has shown that, once a course project is begun, as much time or more is spent on reaching the operational design (the last step in the design phase) as is required for the production, implementation, and evaluation phase that follows.

When the operational diagram is completed for a course, each instructional component or unit has been identified (specific options, remedial units, seminars, large group meetings, and those topics selected for independent study), and the sequence of these units has been determined. In addition, the entire program is placed in a realistic instructional time frame. While modification continues throughout the entire developmental process, the changes beyond this point are usually relatively minor, not significantly affecting the overall design. As a result, it should be possible at the completion of the operational outline to assign the development of specific units to the participating instructional staff if more than one faculty member is involved and to schedule implementation or field testing.

For maximum efficiency, this modification from ideal to operational design will be based on several factors. Since each of these factors directly affects what evolves, each must be explored in detail. With the entire logistics of the instructional program being based on the decisions that are now being made, a lack of attention to detail at this time can be most serious.

Goals. While individual lesson or class objectives are dealt with in the production phase of a project, the major instructional approach of a course must be decided here. If the major focus of a course is on information dissemination, lectures and independent study become the obvious instructional mode. If the major emphasis is on problem solving, instruction will be built around laboratory and small group activities. If speaking skills are to be developed, the time necessary for class presentation must be built into the instructional sequence. The development of interpersonal skills requires time for group meetings and planning. Each type of objective suggests a variety of instructional approaches from which to choose. Gerlach and Ely's (1980) chapter on "Strategies for Teaching" provides a comprehensive guide to selecting the appropriate instructional procedures once the objectives have been specified.

Time. How many hours a week are students available for

instruction, and when are they available? Is there flexibility? Can the fifty-five-minute period be extended? Is there time for independent study? At first, efforts at individualized instruction may create havoc for a registrar, but administrative policies must be flexible enough to serve the academic needs of the program. Unfortunately, this flexibility is sometimes difficult to develop, especially in state systems where "central office" controls may severely limit local administrative flexibility. You must also take into consideration the time students have to complete assignments outside of class and the number of days the students have between classes. The semester, trimester, and quarter systems have specific time structures that have a direct effect on the design of a course. In some, the limited time available between class sessions can severely limit what work can be expected from the students outside the formal classroom.

Resources. Several kinds of resources may be needed and can be utilized. The first is human resources.

Instructional staff: Will the course be taught by a single faculty member or a team? How many faculty are available, and what are their strengths in both subject matter and teaching? If a specific area of required expertise is missing, it may be necessary to use part-time staff "volunteers" or prepackaged, self-contained instructional units. Some faculty are extremely effective in front of a large group; others are more effective as seminar leaders or in handling individual projects. The number of faculty and the competencies of each person will help to determine the design of a program, providing the development team with both options and limitations. If graduate teaching assistants are used in a particular course, a greater number of options can be included. On the other hand, the scope of these options is limited by the academic strengths of the available graduate students. Using transient personnel also means that less responsibility can be delegated and that more time must be spent annually training these individuals and designing student manuals and other support materials.

Other resources: Are individuals outside the formal instructional team available for specific seminars and projects? An English course may be able to get excellent cooperation from faculty in other disciplines to help grade extra-credit papers written in their areas of expertise, and a history course may offer seminars by faculty from the music, art, and literature departments. There are people in the community who will be glad to contribute their expertise to a course at all levels of instruction and in many subject areas, if they are asked. Their aid could range from providing work experiences and formal internships within the business community to serving as guest lecturers and panel members.

The second type of resource is material, from museums and art galleries to traditional instructional materials and techniques. All such resources should be examined for possible use in the course. Are there commercial series or packages of materials that you can use? Commercially available programmed or computer-based units, if effective and if designed for the specific population involved, are ideal for remedial work. In such areas as music, art, literature, and history, there may be related exhibits, concerts, and plays available through the community or from a national source (for example, IBM's Leonardo da Vinci and Old Clocks exhibits). What are the resources available in local libraries and museums? How can they be used for maximum effectiveness?

Space and fiscal support capabilities may also force major changes in the design and content of a program because they cannot meet its logistical needs. How large are the available lecture halls, and can media be used effectively within them? In some instances, it might be necessary to modify development plans substantially if there are not enough seminar rooms available or if the rooms that are needed are not available at key times. In a science course, how many student stations are available, and how are they equipped?

How much money is available for development and implementation? Can some of the new materials be sold to the students, reducing the cost to the department? While these answers will vary from program to program, there is always a dollar constraint within which the project must operate. If disposable materials must be used or a large number of films rented, can a student course fee be instituted? Administrative constraints may require one course to handle more students for the same dollar, a second course may be designed to cut costs, while a third may be set up to improve the educational program by making better use of existing resources.

The final program will, moreover, be affected not only by the total funds available for development and implementation but also by restrictions on how a dollar can be spent. For example, certain dollars may be available only for staffing and personnel, whereas other funds might be limited to the purchase of equipment and materials. The ideal is to have maximum flexibility. The fewer the constraints, the greater the freedom in developing the instructional design. In reality, most funding support from outside sources, particularly from the government, is specifically limited in how and where it can be spent.

In addition, what resources are available once a program becomes operational? It is folly to design a course that cannot continue after its experimental stage due to lack of fiscal support. If a grant supports development, make sure the design can continue after these funds are used up. All too many innovative programs, developed with the help of foundations or governmental support, have died soon after their support was withdrawn because those involved did not design a program that could survive without this material support. Interdisciplinary courses, too, can be a particular problem if the participating faculty are not rewarded for their participation. The excitement of being involved in an innovative project is brief.

Students. The data collected earlier on the students now become a major factor in the overall project design. How many students can be anticipated to enroll, and who are they? What learning experiences have they had, and will additional orientation be required to permit maximum smoothness of course implementation? Are there groups of students with identifiable attitudes, problems, backgrounds, or strengths that should be separated at certain times for specialized instruction? Should special units be included to build on students' interest in a particular field or subject major? How many students can be expected to select certain options, and how many are assigned to particular remedial units? Are there students who have related experiences that suggest they be given exemptions or that they might be used as resource people? Can one accommodate more students by identifying the most capable and exempting them from modules they have already mastered?

The location of the students and their hours of availability can also be significant. Full-time students offer design options that are not possible with a classroom composed of part-time students who are available for only a few hours a week. By the very nature of its structure, a course that is designed to reach students in a primarily independent learning mode must be designed to operate far differently than the standard class. Recognizing the significance of student location in instructional design, van Enckevort, Harry, Morin, and Schutze have devoted an entire section of their book on distance learning (1986) to the learning process and media selection in which distance learning is involved.

Research. Which approaches and techniques work, and which do not? What options do you have? What has been tried elsewhere, and what happened when it was? If things went wrong, why? How are some of these projects the same as the projects being undertaken at other institutions, and how are they different? For example, research on the use of audio cassettes for grading papers will have immediate significance to projects in freshman composition or for faculty working on any course in which a great deal of writing is required. Three excellent sources for research on the various instructional approaches and on the application of technology in teaching are Wilbur J. McKeachie's *Teaching Tips: A Guidebook for the Beginning College Teacher* (1986), *The International Encyclopaedia of Education: Research and Studies* (Husen, 1985), and the ERIC Clearinghouse on Information Resources at Syracuse University.

Unfortunately, we find approaches that are not successful being tried again and again as those involved regard their efforts and skills as unique and consider past results irrelevant. It is a great advantage to utilize existing materials and learn from the experience of others. Although many failures are not reported in detail, it is wise to study related projects. A phone call or letter to those working on a similar project will often prove extremely helpful, and if travel funds are available, a visit to a related project can be very useful. Unfortunately, national recognition does not necessarily correlate with either quality or replicability. In many instances, the recognition a project receives may result more directly from the fact that particular external agencies or foundations support the project than from the quality and practicality of the project itself.

Is a successful project capable of replication, or is success the result of a single, outstanding faculty member? Are there both positive and negative features of a particular technique, and what are they? What have been the experiences, for example, at Michigan State, Brigham Young, Oakland Community College, San Jose State University, and Miami-Dade Junior College, where major course development efforts using instructional technology have been undertaken? What are the strengths and weaknesses of the television efforts at San Jose State University and the State University College at Brockport? What has been the impact of the dial access system at the State University of New York, Fredonia, Oral Roberts University, and Fulton-Montgomery Junior College in Johnstown, New York, and are they still being used? How useful and cost effective are the interactive video units being developed at University College (University of Maryland) and Utah State University? Has the investment in computers for instructional purposes at Arizona State University, Florida State University, the University of Illinois, the University of Indiana, and the University of Minnesota met expectations? What has the Center for Educational Practice at the University of Guelph, Ontario, Canada, learned about the use of teleconferencing in instruction? Is the evaluation approach being used most successfully at Alverno College transferable to larger campuses with more heterogeneous student populations? In any project a number of such questions should be addressed before the design of the program is completed.

Capitalize on the successes and failures of other institutions, and use existing materials whenever they meet your needs. Not to do so is an absurd waste of time, talent, and resources.

Grading and Scheduling Options. The grading system may also have to be revised if new credit structures and time frames are to be implemented—an additional problem for the registrar, and, if it is used, the computer center. Minicourses and credit options require an administrative system that can allow additional credits to be earned and easily recorded. One way to maximize schedule flexibility is to block schedule a course as was done in the Introduction to the Study of Religion project described in Chapter Five. A subject may traditionally be taught three hours a week, but scheduling it twice weekly for two hours greatly increases the number of possible options, since such a schedule presumes that every student can attend any meeting at that hour either day. This schedule, for example, permits the use of both two-hour classes or one-hour sessions running back to back. When nontraditional scheduling is planned, it is important to explain to the student that while a course may be scheduled four or five hours a week, he or she will not be required to attend all these sessions. In addition, the amount of time that each instructional unit is allocated must be established within the total time allotted for the semester. If a continuous registration system, flexible credit, or the flexible use of space makes sense for the project, get the registrar involved early. If, as noted earlier, the decision makers have some ownership of the project, they can prove to be amazingly helpful.

As these factors are explored, it is possible to outline the course as it will actually be implemented. At this stage, expect changes to be modest. During the preliminary design period, major additions and deletions and changes in content are common; these adjustments will usually represent fine tuning. The development of the philosophy course described below traces such adjustments.

Case Study: Philosophy

Figures 20 and 21 diagram an introductory philosophy course, Writing and Philosophical Analysis. This course was developed specifically to permit students to meet the continuing writing requirements of the then new Arts and Sciences Core Curriculum. Notice how the writing emphasis has been built into the entire fabric of the course. The two drafts represent the

Figure 20. Philosophy 102: Writing/Philosophical Analysis Sequence Outline — Draft 3.

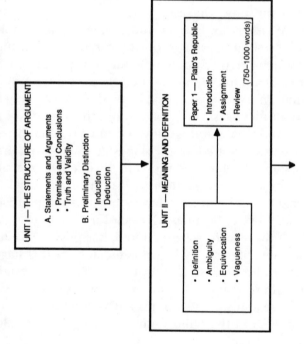

UNIT I — THE STRUCTURE OF ARGUMENT

A. Statements and Arguments
   • Premises and Conclusions
   • Truth and Validity

B. Preliminary Distinction
   • Induction
   • Deduction

UNIT II — MEANING AND DEFINITION

• Definition
• Ambiguity
• Equivocation
• Vagueness

Paper 1 — Plato's Republic
   • Introduction
   • Assignment
   • Review
   (750–1000 words)

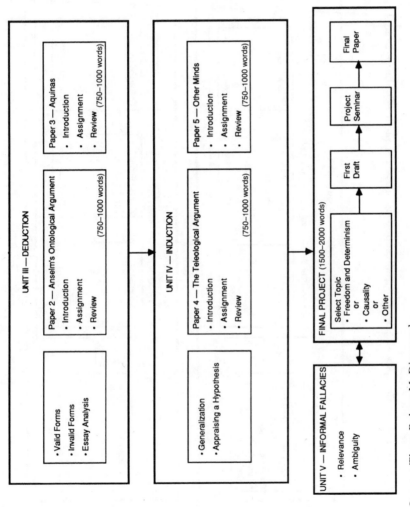

UNIT III — DEDUCTION

- Valid Forms
- Invalid Forms
- Essay Analysis

Paper 2 — Anselm's Ontological Argument
- Introduction
- Assignment
- Review   (750–1000 words)

Paper 3 — Aquinas
- Introduction
- Assignment
- Review   (750–1000 words)

UNIT IV — INDUCTION

- Generalization
- Appraising a Hypothesis

Paper 4 — The Teleological Argument
- Introduction
- Assignment
- Review   (750–1000 words)

Paper 5 — Other Minds
- Introduction
- Assignment
- Review   (750–1000 words)

UNIT V — INFORMAL FALLACIES
- Relevance
- Ambiguity

FINAL PROJECT (1500–2000 words)

Select Topic
- Freedom and Determinism
  or
- Causality
  or
- Other

First Draft

Project Seminar

Final Paper

Source: Stewart Thau, Robert M. Diamond.

Figure 21. Philosophy 102: Writing/Philosophical Analysis Sequence Outline—Draft 4.

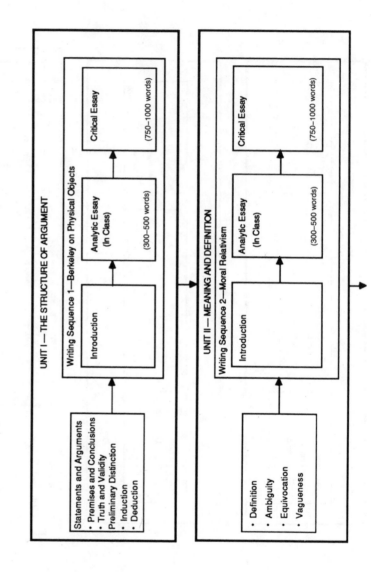

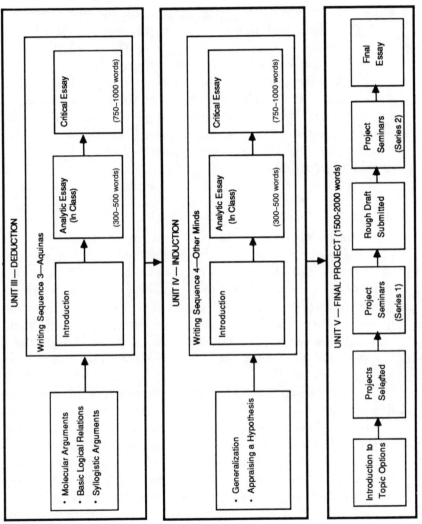

UNIT III — DEDUCTION

Writing Sequence 3—Aquinas

- Molecular Arguments
- Basic Logical Relations
- Syllogistic Arguments

Introduction

Analytic Essay
(In Class)

(300–500 words)

Critical Essay

(750–1000 words)

UNIT IV — INDUCTION

Writing Sequence 4—Other Minds

- Generalization
- Appraising a Hypothesis

Introduction

Analytic Essay
(In Class)

(300–500 words)

Critical Essay

(750–1000 words)

UNIT V — FINAL PROJECT (1500–2000 words)

Introduction to
Topic Options

Projects
Selected

Project
Seminars
(Series 1)

Rough Draft
Submitted

Project
Seminars
(Series 2)

Final
Essay

Source: Stewart Thau, Robert M. Diamond.

changes that took place in a single design meeting. Notice how in units II, III, and IV the instructional sequence has become more clearly defined, whereas one section in Unit III has been eliminated to reduce the grading load on the instructor. In addition, while the number of papers has been increased, the length of many has been reduced. By the end of draft 4, the focus and type of essay have also been determined.

While some minor modifications sometimes occur in the design of a course or curriculum during the production stage that follows, most of the remaining changes take place after field testing or initial implementation. These later adjustments are based on the data collected during the initial offering of the new or revised programs.

Summary

In this chapter we discussed moving from the ideal to a potentially operational program. In this and in the preceding chapters, we looked at a number of courses and curricula. While some of these are traditional in design, others, such as religion, freshman English, and cost effectiveness, are somewhat unusual in their concept and structure. It is interesting to note that although these courses vary substantially in design and sequencing, each was produced using the same instructional development model.

After the operational sequence is complete, production, implementation, and evaluation can begin. A major advantage of this approach, when more than one faculty member is involved, is that once the operational elements of the instructional sequence are identified, many of the specific units can be developed simultaneously, facilitating implementation. This is possible since each unit has general objectives, an operational time frame, and a clear relationship to the other components. The number of units that can be undertaken at one time is limited only by the number of faculty that are available for the purpose.

The following checklist of items should be considered in developing the operational design of curriculum and course projects.

1. Curriculum projects
   - Accreditation requirements
   - Credit restrictions
   - Fiscal and staff constraints
   - Effectiveness of existing courses/programs
2. Course projects
   - Goals
   - Time—faculty availability for instruction and other course-related activities
   - Resources: people (instructional staff/others), material, facilities, fiscal resources
   - Students: number, backgrounds, goals, location
   - Research (instructional tools and techniques)
   - Grading and scheduling options: continuous registration, flexible credit

In the chapters that follow, we will discuss implementation of the course that has now been designed.

7

Clarifying
Instructional Objectives
and Assessing Outcomes

This chapter discusses the requirement for stating instructional objectives in performance terms, relates objectives to assessment, describes the qualities of well-written objectives, and introduces an efficient and effective way of developing them. The chapter concludes with a discussion of the relationship between student objectives and evaluation procedures and a review of the roles of evaluation in course improvement.

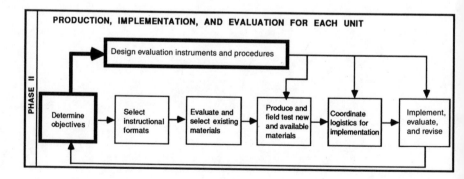

Overview

Once the outline of a course is complete, the production, implementation, and evaluation activities begin. During this phase

- objectives are specified
- evaluation procedures and instruments are developed
- methods or strategies of instruction are chosen
- materials are selected and/or developed
- new units/materials are field tested (when possible)
- the program is implemented, evaluated, and, when needed, revised

In addition, during this phase some further changes in the operational design should be anticipated. While these modifications are usually minor, their impact on the overall success of the project can be significant. These changes usually take place in two areas—time and content. Time adjustments occur when it becomes clear that the specified objectives will not be reached in the time allotted. As a result, some objectives and content may be eliminated or modified while other units are given more time for completion. Even after implementation, most courses undergo fine tuning as identified problems are addressed, changes occur in the discipline, units are corrected, changes are made in the content, or new faculty with different strengths and backgrounds enter the program. In this chapter, we will focus on the first steps of this phase—determining objectives and designing evaluation instruments and procedures.

As the team moves through these activities, it is important to take care that the broader, more general goals of the course are dealt with and built into the objectives of the individual course. These nondiscipline-specific objectives exist within every course and focus on those skills and competencies that every student needs to succeed after graduation—the ability to write and speak effectively, the ability to work well with others, and so on.

Objectives and Assessment

A report by the National Institute of Education, *Involvement in Learning: Realizing the Potential of American Higher Education* (1984), called for increased emphasis on undergraduate teaching and learning and concluded "that institutions should be accountable, not only for stating their expectations and standards, but for assessing the degree to which these ends have been met" (p. 21). This report, along with a number of other major publications, focused the nation's attention on problems associated with the performance of the American system of higher education and led directly to a movement toward a more direct legislative role in higher education. Another report, *Transforming the State Role in Undergraduate Education: Time for a Different View* (1986), from the Education Commission of the States, not only stressed the importance of undergraduate education for economic and international development but challenged the states to take a direct and active role in improving the assessment of students. In the same year, the National Governors' Association recommended that comprehensive assessment programs be developed jointly by institutions and state governments or coordinating boards.

A major assessment movement is under way in higher education. The key to whether or not it will have the desired positive effect rests directly on five factors: (1) the quality of the goals that are developed, (2) how well these broader goals are stated on an operational basis in performance terms, (3) whether or not these same goals are transferred to course-specific goals, (4) the match between the objectives and the assessment instruments that are used (at all levels of instruction), and (5) the involvement and ownership that individual faculty and academic departments have in the overall effort. Unless all five of these elements are taken into consideration, the assessment movement will not have its desired outcome, and the overall process can become disruptive, causing friction among faculty and administrators and between administrators and state officials. What was originally hoped to be a positive factor can, if the process is not implemented with great care, become a negative force on the very institutions its proponents hope to improve. In addition, those behind the assessment movement must recognize that assessment is only one important element in the academic program, and that this approach is only as good as the quality and specificity of the objectives that appear at the program and individual classroom levels. However ambitious the institutional goals, the quality of the improvement in higher education is determined at the point at which instruction takes place and at which faculty and students work together in the educational process. As Theodore J. Marchese (1987, p. 8) in his review of the assessment movement writes, "Assessment *per se* guarantees nothing by way of improvement, no more than a thermometer cures a fever. Only when used in *combination* with good instruction (that evokes involvement in coherent curricula, etc.) in a program of improvement, can the device strengthen education."

Stating Objectives

An Overview

Robert F. Mager (1975) tells the story of a sea horse who, with money in hand, swims off to seek his fortune. After purchasing flippers and a jet-propelled scooter to speed up his travels, he comes across a shark. The shark informs him that if the sea horse swims into the shark's mouth, the sea horse will find his fortune. The sea horse follows this advice and is never heard from again. The moral of this fable is that if you are not sure where you are going, you are liable to end up someplace you do not want to be.

There is little question that, if we are to determine whether or not academic programs are successful, we must initially determine the goals of academic programs, courses, and curricula. We must state in specific terms what we expect the students to be able to do and then determine whether or not, at the completion of the instructional process, they can reach these goals. This standard requires that we describe goals or objectives in performance terms and that evaluation instruments and procedures adequately assess the abilities of students to meet specific criteria.

In addition to forming the base upon which external assessment programs must be designed, providing students with clearly stated objectives offers significant advantages at the course and program levels.

- Fairness of both testing and grading is facilitated.
- Goals of the course, content, and evaluation procedures are both consistent and interrelated.
- Course and materials evaluation identify what is effective and working and what is not.
- Orientation from "what I (as a faculty member) must cover" is changed to what a student should be able to do as a consequence of instruction.
- A logical and effective instructional sequence is communicated by identifying a sequence of objectives and thus content; that is, the student must first be able to do *a* before he or she can do *b*.
- Communication between and among faculty and support staff is improved.
- Self-evaluation by the students is encouraged since they know what is expected of them.
- Efficient student learning is facilitated, and anxiety is reduced by providing direction and identifying instructional priorities.

If stating objectives in performance terms is so vitally important, why has the assessment movement met with such limited acceptance twenty years after this approach was first introduced into education? The answer lies in what it required and how it was introduced.

In their report on over eighty instructionally related projects, Bergquist and Armstrong (1986) note that stating goals in performance terms was a major problem area in these programs. "While viewed by the architects of Project QUE (Quality Undergraduate Education) as the foundation of academic planning, the outcomes approach was one of the more controversial elements of the project. The crux of the challenge was aptly described by one campus coordinator (who chose to remain anonymous): 'The major shift to describing program goals in terms of student outcomes... required effort on the part of faculty, most of whom had conceptualized their teaching in terms of their content area rather than with reference to student outcomes'" (p. 82).

The authors concluded, however, that while focusing on the results of learning did not gain total acceptance among the several hundred faculty and administrators who were involved, the approach was viewed at the end of the project as being both practical and essential by the majority of the participants.

Unfortunately, the use of the term *behavioral objectives* was a second major hurdle to overcome. The way the approach was introduced to many of the faculty who were most open to experimentation and change has often deterred its acceptance. Ohmer Milton (Milton and Associates, 1978, p. 3), in reviewing Robert M. Barry's (1978) excellent chapter on clarifying objectives, writes, "in my judgment the weakest area of classroom instruction is that of specifying course objectives. He [Barry] quite properly avoids the unwarranted simplicity of much that is written about college course objectives—a simplicity especially true of many treatises about 'behavioral objectives.' All too often, this concept has been carried to ridiculous extremes and has earned a resulting contempt."

Because many of the early advocates of stating goals in performance terms focused on minutiae and on complex classification systems, they, not surprisingly, "turned off" the very people they were hoping to convert. Horror stories from these early efforts still abound. No wonder that the State of New Jersey (State of New Jersey College Outcomes Evaluation Program Advisory Committee, 1987), as it developed its statewide assessment program, diligently avoided using the term *behavioral objectives*, focusing instead on college "outcomes." However, student performance by any other name is still a behavioral objective.

However important course and curricular goals may be, the need is to develop statements that are useful to the faculty member and to the student: objectives that are clear and concise

Figure 22. Hierarchy of Objective Specificity.

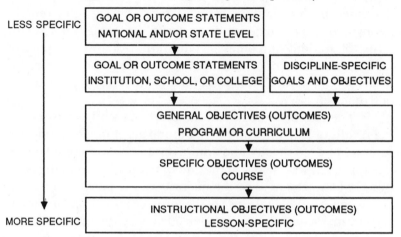

Source: Robert M. Diamond.

and that can be measured within the framework of the instructional unit.

Before course-specific objectives can be written, there are times when reference must be made to other statements created by the college, university, or state. This will become more common as state departments of education provide specific goal statements and require implementation of assessment programs on campuses under their control. As goal statements move from the national and state levels, to the college/university, to the school or college, to the curriculum, and finally, to the course, they must become more specific and, in most instances, more easily measured (see Figure 22). As noted previously, in almost every course, nondiscipline-specific goals must be both addressed and measured.

For example, the Task Force on the Student Experience of the Faculty of Arts and Sciences, Rutgers University, Newark, New Jersey, recently completed a list of the competencies they felt would describe the "Qualities of the Liberally Educated Person" (see Resource C). The qualities, characteristics, abilities, or competencies in this list are stated in terms that can be observed and measured. However, as the following examples demonstrate, these characteristics are still written in a form that requires additional specification before student performance can be assessed.

Under the category of "scientific reasoning" are a number of competency statements, including

1. [The student] demonstrates an understanding of the scientific method of inquiry, including accurate measurement based on observation and the use of controlled experiment.
2. [The student] identifies the assumptions and limitations of the scientific method of inquiry and distinguishes the extent to which this method is applicable in various situations and contexts in all disciplines and fields of inquiry (see Resource C).

Since individual courses are the vehicles for developing many of these competencies, it would be the responsibility of faculty to include within their statements of course objectives both those objectives that are content- and discipline-specific and those from the broader list that are appropriate. In these two instances, the faculty would have to take these statements and rewrite them in the terms of the specific course they were teaching. This would require describing how the student should demonstrate "an understanding of the scientific method of inquiry" (Objective 1) or asking the student to "identify the assumptions and limitations of the scientific method" in an applied context (Objective 2).

Writing an Objective. To be useful, an objective must contain three basic elements:

- a verb that describes an observable action
- a description of the conditions under which this action takes place—"when given *x* you will be able to. . ."
- the level of acceptable performance—that is, what percentage of correct answers will be considered acceptable, how many errors will be permitted, how many and which examples must be included, and so on

In addition, if the sequence or unit is to be used with other students, it is essential that the learner for whom the material is designed be described and prerequisites identified. It is important that the words used to describe student behavior in these objectives be clear, concise, and not open to misinterpretation. Robert Mager (1975) provides the following suggestions of terms to avoid and to use.

Words Open to Many Interpretations	*Words Open to Fewer Interpretations*
to know	to write
to understand	to recite
to *really* understand	to identify
to appreciate	to sort
to *fully* appreciate	to solve
to grasp the significance of	to construct
to enjoy	to build
to believe	to compare
to have faith in	to contrast
to internalize	to smile

Categorizing Objectives. While there are almost as many ways of categorizing objectives as there are authors of textbooks on the subject, the use of such a system at the course level is questionable. At the state, institutional, or curriculum level, some organization is essential for the material to be useful. It will be up to the writers of these statements to select the system that they feel most comfortable with. However, experience has shown that it is rarely cost effective for faculty to spend a great deal of time analyzing the type or level of their objectives. It is far more essential that an effort be made to ensure that useful statements be written, that they include all of the elements that should be addressed, and that they be measurable within the context of the course.

Other Factors. There are instances when the overall objective focuses more on process than on the ability of the student to reach a specific outcome. In their discussion on the testing of a conceptualization of a value, Krathwohl, Bloom, and Masia (1964, p. 157) write, "The process of conceptualization is largely cognitive, involving abstraction and generalization . . . the emphasis is less on the *quality* of the cognitive process than on the fact that they are being used."

In these instances the faculty member might use examples in which there are no right or wrong answers and ask the student to express a point of view. For evaluation purposes, focus is then on the process used, the alternatives explored, and the student's justification for the conclusion. At other times the student might be asked to list a number of alternative solutions to a problem and then to defend the solution selected.

Finally, faculty must write their own objectives. While a course may fulfill the requirements of others (professional agencies, boards of trustees, the university, or the department), the objectives must be developed to satisfy the instructor(s) responsible for instruction.

An Almost Painless Way of Specifying Objectives. When faculty are asked point-blank to state their "instructional" or "behavioral" objectives, several things occur. First, they tend to resent the question; second, they produce far more objectives than could ever be used; and, third, most of these objectives are at a trivial level, since they are the easiest to write. In addition, this process has a tendency to disenchant a large number of faculty, as it is time-consuming, often boring, and usually frustrating. As a helpful alternative to writing objectives in the abstract, the instructional developer may play the role of the student and ask the faculty member(s), "If I'm your student, what do I have to do to convince you that I'm where you want me to be at the end of this lesson (unit or course)?" Out of this discussion will come objectives that are measurable in performance terms and that tend to be far more important and at a higher level than would be produced otherwise. In addition, this process, while difficult at times, is generally comfortable and efficient, and the specific statements that are needed for the development of projects are produced.

Representative Samples of Objectives. A sampling of objectives from various courses follows. Note that each of these examples is written directly to the student, answers the question "What must the student do to prove that he or she has succeeded?", and identifies what the student must be given *before* this question can be answered.

- *Statistics:* When given two events, you will be able to determine if they are independent or if there is a relationship
between them (that is, if one event affects the probability of
the other). On the basis of this decision, you will be able to
select and use the appropriate rules of conditional probability to determine the probability that a certain event will
occur.
- *Religion:* When given a definition of the term *religion*, you will
be able to identify which of the following characteristics is
emphasized—feeling, ritual activity, belief, monotheism, the
solitary individual, social valuation, illusion, ultimate reality, and value.
- *Music:* Upon hearing musical selections, you will be able to
identify those that are examples of chamber music and
be able to identify the form, texture, and makeup of the
ensemble.
- *Art* (general introduction): When shown a print, you will be
able to identify whether it is a woodcut, an etching, or a
lithograph, and you will be able to list the characteristics on
which this decision was based.
- *Psychology:* When given a case study, you will be able to
identify whether or not it describes a case of schizophrenia
and, if it does, which of the following schizophrenic reac-
tions are involved—hebephrenic, catatonic, or paranoid.

These objectives help students clarify the goals they ought to set for themselves, improve their studying efficiency, and reduce their anxiety, and they provide an opportunity for faculty to determine how successful they have been as teachers. As a final step, the faculty member would, for evaluation purposes, establish a standard or level of performance for each of the various levels of grading being used. In some instances, this would involve combining objectives and questions to measure overall performance.

Limitations of Objectives. In order to avoid discouraging

some faculty and alienating others, keep in mind the limitations of objectives.

Some objectives or goals cannot be measured within existing time and program limitations. In art and music, for example, a secondary goal may be to develop, in the student, viewing and listening habits that will last throughout a lifetime. These goals are not measurable within the framework of a single course or even a total four-year academic program. What the instructor must do is select as objectives the skills, knowledge, and attitudes that he or she believes will result in the desired behavior. The evaluation focus must be on the objectives that fit within the scope of the course.

Behavioral objectives need not be low-level cognitive skills. Many faculty have come to equate a behavioral objective with a multiple-choice, true-false, or similar selected-response format. This misconception is unfortunate as well as incorrect. Objectives legitimately can include changes in attitude and in performance skills. The students' abilities to relate philosophies to concepts and to defend their answers, to relate history to current events, to design a structure or write an article that meets prestated criteria, and to perform cooperatively within a small group are examples of valid higher-order instructional outcomes that can be measured.

When overused, behavioral objectives can limit creativity and reduce instructional excitement. Instructional objectives should provide us with a basis for evaluating performance ranging from minimum competence to more advanced levels of knowledge, attitudes, and performance. The process of developing and testing for specific objectives is important, but it should not preclude flexibility and, as opportunities arise, addressing new elements. In addition, the larger goals of a course must always be kept in view. For example, while the objective might never appear on a quiz or a final examination, a primary goal of a course may be to excite the students about a subject area or field of study.

This is not to suggest that we should eliminate performance-based objectives but to emphasize that, although they may be necessary, they have inherent limitations that must be recognized as one develops and uses objectives.

Designing Evaluation Instruments and Procedures

By the end of this step, all major objectives should be stated and listed for each instructional unit. Once we have reached this point, work can begin simultaneously in two areas: (1) the selection and design of the evaluation procedures and instruments that are necessary to implement the course and to determine the success of the students and the course and (2) the production of the instructional units themselves.

Based on the objectives that have been developed and the overall structure of the course, it now becomes possible to design procedures and instruments that serve four distinct purposes.

1. Identify those students who may require remediation or receive exemption (diagnostic tests). This requires a clear statement of anticipated student prerequisites and the design of an instrument or procedure that tests for these specific abilities. Tests of this type must be very specific to permit remedial assignments to be made on the basis of individual need. Most tests used for course placement are too general for this purpose.

2. Measure student performance—whether the objectives (individual units and entire courses) are being met. This includes the measurement of newly acquired skills, knowledge, and attitudes. It is crucial that there be a perfect fit between the stated objectives, the content of the course, and the student evaluation instruments that will be used. All too often the objectives that are given to the students have little in common with either the content of the course or the questions that are asked on the tests and examinations. Unless all three elements are closely interrelated, significant functional problems will develop, and the students will become frustrated and antagonized.

3. Measure students' attitudes toward the course and the disci-

pline or field. Some courses have, as an unstated objective, the goal of improving the attitude of the student toward the field or profession. Questions that collect attitudinal data can, for comparison purposes, be built into course orientation activities and then into end-of-course evaluations.

4. Measure the efficiency and effectiveness of the overall course design and the materials and procedures that are being used. Survey instruments used near the end of a course can collect useful data on pacing, interest, structure, and overall design.

Remember, the more specific the performance expected from students, the fewer the problems that appear in developing student testing instruments and procedures. Appropriate testing and evaluation procedures should be used, ranging from the traditional multiple-choice, matching, and essay questions to observing student performance while using a predetermined set of criteria. While some of these methods may take more time and effort than others, not using them would be unfair to the student and would also represent, in the long run, a reduction in quality of the total instructional program. McKeachie (1986) provides an excellent review of the various types of tests, their uses, and design and discusses in some detail test administration, grading, and scoring.

It is important to keep in mind that student evaluation at the course level has two functions.

1. It provides data on individual student performance for grading purposes.
2. It provides data on the overall effectiveness of instruction, identifying those areas that may require revising and/or improvement.

A number of these instruments and procedures will be used not only during the actual teaching of the courses but during the field testing of specific instructional activities and materials. In Chapter Ten, there are case studies describing the collection and use of such data.

8

Selecting
and Developing
Instructional Media

This chapter focuses on the design of instruction, the selection of media, and the need for administrative concern about logistics. Individualized learning is defined, and several instructional management systems are introduced and compared.

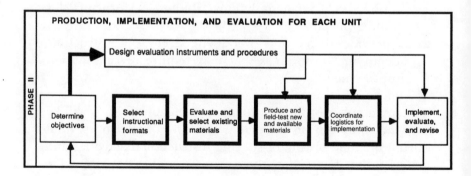

Overview

By the time this stage in the design process has been reached, decisions regarding the overall structure of the course have been made. There is general agreement as to whether the course will include diagnostic testing, remediation, or exemption; whether it will be self-paced; whether it will use lectures, seminars, or independent study; if it is to be a laboratory; and whether it will include work experiences. In addition, the overall topics of each unit are known, as are whether or not they are sequential and whether students are to have the opportunity to select options or tracks of specialization.

By now, decisions have determined the number or range of credits that will be offered, in which semester(s) the course will be taught, and, in general, how much time will be available for instruction. In courses in which more than one faculty member is involved, it has been determined what their role(s) will be. For example, answers will have been reached to such questions as whether the course will be team-taught with faculty sharing the responsibility for lectures or whether each will teach separate, independent sections. If graduate teaching assistants are involved, their role has been defined. For example, will they handle recitation sections in the laboratory portion of the course, or will they be responsible for delivering some of the lectures or only for grading and counseling?

At this point in the design process, these broader decisions will become more clearly defined as specifics are dealt with unit by unit, lesson by lesson.

Format Selection

The design team will now have to decide, on a unit-by-unit basis, how to structure each unit in the course. This decision depends on a number of factors including

- the number and quality of the students,
- the instructional objectives of the unit,

Figure 23. Selecting Structural Options for Each Instructional Component.

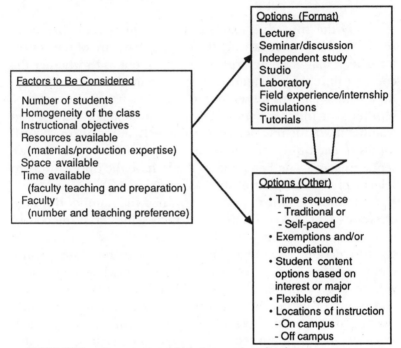

Options (Format)

Lecture
Seminar/discussion
Independent study
Studio
Laboratory
Field experience/internship
Simulations
Tutorials

Factors to Be Considered

Number of students
Homogeneity of the class
Instructional objectives
Resources available
  (materials/production expertise)
Space available
Time available
  (faculty teaching and preparation)
Faculty
  (number and teaching preference)

Options (Other)

• Time sequence
  - Traditional or
  - Self-paced
• Exemptions and/or
  remediation
• Student content
  options based on
  interest or major
• Flexible credit
• Locations of instruction
  - On campus
  - Off campus

REMEMBER: • Any course can include a number of options.
                 • Options may be selected on a unit-by-unit basis.

- the resources available (instructional media options, production assistance, dollars for the purchase of new items),
- the time available for teaching, for assignments between lessons, for the production of new materials, and
- the individual strengths and preferences of the faculty.

The range of these factors and the options available are extensive (see Figure 23). As noted in the figure, the development team must finally decide if the overall course or elements within it will be traditional or self-paced, whether or not to make available exemptions or remediation on the basis of diagnostic testing, and whether students are to be allowed to elect specialized content options during the course.

Many of the case studies included in this book show that

each of these structure options operates most effectively under certain circumstances.

Self-pacing enables students to progress through a course or part of a course at their own rate on the basis of their ability to pass a specific unit or section test, requires that the content be sequential, is most effective when students can be expected to learn at significantly different rates, and requires excellent instructional materials designed specifically for independent study and the availability of one-on-one counseling or tutoring.

Exemption and/or remediation exempts students from parts or units of a course or assigns additional work to correct a deficiency on the basis of their entering competencies. It is most useful when prerequisite problems exist or when it is anticipated that some students will have had prior course work or experience in the area, and it requires a quality testing program and well-designed remedial instruction (independent study using computer-based or programmed units may be used effectively for this purpose).

Content option gives students a choice among assignments that are all designed to meet the same learning objective. These assignments range from giving the students the opportunity to write about a topic in their major area to using the same model to solve a problem of their choice. The content option is most effective when the class is composed of students with specific interests that can be related to the content or goals of the course.

Flexible credit allows students enrolled in the same course to earn different numbers of credits based either on additional units they are required to take or on extra work they do at their discretion. Flexible credit can be used effectively both in remedial courses in which assignments are made on the basis of need and in advanced or honors courses in which certain students may wish to do extra work for extra credit. It is suggested that flexible credit systems permit each credit to be graded independently and listed in this way on the student's transcript.

In making these decisions there are always trade-offs. For example, the need for self-pacing can limit the use of large group meetings, but the availability of an outstanding lecturer may make it worthwhile to build in a number of large group sessions, limiting somewhat the flexibility needed for individualization. If students enter a course with academic deficiencies, these gaps must be closed by remediation if these students are to succeed. Of course, remediation requires time, which means that other elements of the course may have to be adjusted, and unless the remedial assignments are "add-ons" outside of class, plans have to be made to accommodate the students who do not require these remedial activities.

The decisions that are made at this time determine the structure of the course and also identify the role of the faculty. In some instances that role may be more managerial than instructional.

Managerial Systems

Over the past two decades several major management systems have been widely used. The first is the audiotutorial approach implemented in 1961 by Samuel Postlethwait (Postlethwait, Novak, and Murray, 1972) in his freshman botany course at Purdue University. A second is the "Keller Plan" (Keller, 1968), which gives the student an opportunity to move from unit to unit as soon as he or she is able to meet a specific criterion (above 80 percent, 90 percent, and so on) on individual unit tests. This approach to testing is called "Mastery Learning" and has been used on a large number of subjects, usually at the lower-division level. Unfortunately, there has been a tendency to equate both these approaches with individualized instruction. A comparison of both plans — in most ways they are similar — with a comprehensive definition of individualized instruction reveals the following:

Elements of Individualization Included in These Approaches

1. Flexible time frames for completion
2. Stress on independent study
3. Review session to meet specific problems

Elements of Individualization Usually Missing in These Approaches

1. Diagnostic evaluation of prerequisites followed by remediation and exemptions

2.   Content options based on interest and/or need
3.   Flexible sequencing (when appropriate)
4.   Alternate evaluation techniques
5.   Alternate instructional techniques

The two approaches have specific differences between them that must also be considered as the two management systems are explored. Although both are generally linear in design—that is, every student follows the same learning sequence—the Keller Plan can be adapted to the branching concept more easily because of its more flexible approach to media. (In the branching concept, students follow different sequences that are determined by their answers to questions within the instructional material.) In addition, the audiotutorial technique has generally been designed "around" a specific faculty member and as a result is often extremely difficult to replicate in its entirety from campus to campus or even from instructor to instructor.

Several of the courses described as case studies in Chapters Four and Five do include excellent management systems. The freshman writing course, the introductory course on religion, introductory economics, and the self-paced calculus courses all require effective management systems. What separates these from the Keller and Postlethwait approaches are that they tend to combine a number of instructional approaches and the management system was established *after* the course was designed, thinking in the ideal to meet the specific need of that program. Faculty who have adopted the audiotutorial and Keller programs tend to select the management system first and then design the courses around these systems.

Media Selection

After objectives have been established and the mode(s) of instruction determined, it becomes possible to select the specific instructional media, if any. Now available in almost any combination are

1. Audio recordings (tape and record)
2. Video tapes (reel or cassette) or video discs
3. Film (silent and sound)
4. Slides and slide tapes
5. Filmstrips (which may be cut up and used as slides for flexibility)
6. Programmed texts (linear and branching)
7. Workbooks, charts, graphs, illustrations, and so on
8. Microcomputers and programs
9. Interactive video (using video tape, laser disc, or video disc)

Each medium has obvious advantages and, in some instances, major limitations. Final selection is based on such factors as the instructional objectives of the unit; the need for color, motion, or sound; whether or not it will be used for independent study or with a lecture; if self-pacing is desired, cost, availability, ease of use. A comparison of media for use in independent study is found in Figure 24; selection is based on design flexibility (potential for individualization) and cost. Note that, with one or two exceptions, the more expensive a medium is the less flexible it is.

Kemp (1985) has placed this selection in perspective by identifying factors that must be considered in selecting media for traditional instruction, self-paced learning, or small group interaction (see Figure 25). Unfortunately, the glamour of the technology can be very tempting, but wiser selections are based on the rational approach presented here. Excellent technologies require the support of high-quality software. Television, radio, and computer-assisted instruction have all been tarnished by unrealistic expectations followed by improper use and lack of quality control.

Experience has shown that the easier a sequence is to use, the more effective it will generally be. For example, programmed booklets written in a branching format and used alone or with other media are proving most effective in a number of projects. Students like them and they are extremely efficient to use and easy and inexpensive to produce. The internal structure of programmed booklets also makes meeting the

Figure 24. Instructional Media for Use in Independent Study.

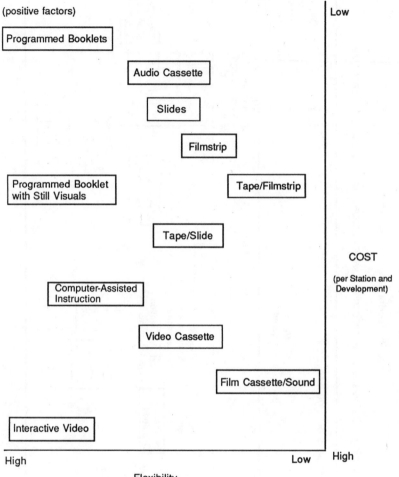

unique needs of students easier as they progress through a programmed sequence. Unfortunately, the poor quality of many of the early programmed materials created negative attitudes toward this excellent approach, attitudes that are still held by many educators.

Programmed booklets or manuals have been used for such diverse purposes as

Figure 25. Media Selection Diagram.

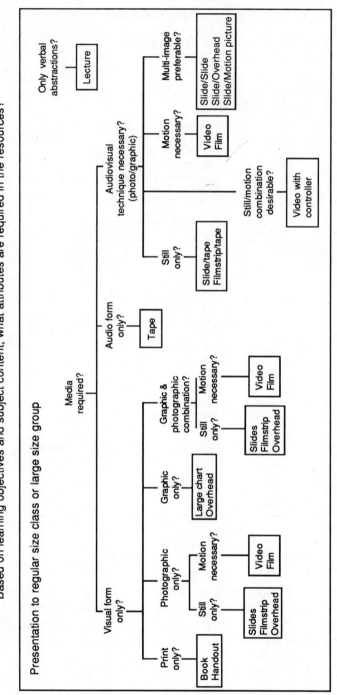

Source: Kemp, 1985, p. 139.

- To teach basic vocabulary in a retailing course
- To introduce inexperienced students and staff to the basic use and operation of various microcomputers (the IBM PC, the Macintosh Apple 2C)
- To teach design students the use of basic drawing instruments
- To teach nonart majors to recognize the various printmaking techniques
- To correct basic math deficiencies in economics students
- To teach management students how to use a complex computerized accounting system
- To teach basic clerical skills to nursing students

The comments of some of the students who went through the printmaking sequence indicate the response of students to this approach when it is done well.

- This was of tremendous help to me. I say this because art has always been a bit confusing in that I looked but never really understood what I was seeing.
- I felt that this is a much easier way to learn the characteristics of art. If you do make a mistake, you find out exactly what was incorrect and why.
- I felt this technique of presenting the elements of art far more effective than the lecture form. I gained much knowledge from the experience as well as truly enjoying myself.

Keep in mind we are not proposing that an entire course necessarily be presented in the same format. Ideally, each course should use whatever medium or combination of media makes sense. Quite often the most effective courses use a number of approaches and instructional techniques.

Case Study: Art History

At San Jose State University, as on most campuses, the introductory art history course for nonmajors, with an enrollment of over 300 students each semester, was taught using the large lecture format, in which the instructor shows slides (often at an extremely rapid pace) and presents information about them and the students, under low-light conditions, observe and try to keep up with their note taking. Rarely with this format is there time for either questions or discussions. Evaluations in these courses tend to focus on the recall of factual information with a heavy emphasis on multiple-choice, true-false, or short-answer questions.

Dissatisfied with the results, one of the faculty members teaching the course (Kathy Cohen) asked Instructional Development Services, a unit of the institution's Faculty and Instructional Development Office, for their help in overcoming a number of concerns. First, she felt her lectures, which tended to be of the same general format from session to session, were monotonous. Second, the students were neither motivated nor interested, and third, their overall performance was far from satisfactory. Her question was a basic one: How might she improve the attitudes and performances of her students while providing them with both an understanding and an appreciation of the artists?

Goals. After a number of discussions between staff of the support unit and the instructor, five general goals for the project evolved.

1. To improve student interest in the subject
2. To improve student learning
3. To develop in the students a positive attitude toward artists and their work
4. To accomplish this by involving the students more actively in the learning process
5. To make teaching the course more intellectually stimulating for the instructor

Fiscal Support. The Faculty and Instructional Development Office also assisted the faculty member in writing a successful grant application to the New Program Development and Evaluation Office in the California State University Chancellor's Office. The $20,000 that was received provided released time for the instructor (one full semester), a graduate student to help gather materials, and the funds necessary to purchase the films and equipment needed for implementation and to produce a variety of instructional materials.

The Design. Recognizing the logistics problem faced by one instructor teaching a large number of students, the design team decided to combine several instructional formats to facilitate both the delivery of information and the active involvement of students. The course that evolved included three major instructional elements: large group sessions, an audiotutorial independent learning laboratory, and small group discussion sections.

1. *Large group sessions* (ninety students each): During these sessions, general announcements are made, tests are taken, and each week the students view a thirty-minute film from Kenneth Clarke's *Civilization* series that places the art being studied into the broader perspective of history and culture. In most instances, these sessions last from thirty-five to forty minutes.
2. *Audiotutorial independent learning laboratory:* Designed for self-paced learning, the laboratory contains twenty student stations equipped with a filmstrip viewer and an audio cassette player. Each week students are required to view two filmstrips while listening to two associated forty-minute discussions on audio cassette. To permit the students to follow the discussion and to make comparisons, the filmstrip frames are numbered and, when appropriate, split screen images are used.
3. *Small group discussion sections:* These sessions, for fifteen to eighteen students, are structured to provide the students with an opportunity to discuss the relationships among the film, the filmstrips, and the text.

While the instructor moves from discussion group to discussion group, the sections are led by graduate students who also supervise the learning laboratory. These students, who are planning to become art teachers, receive three "special studies" credits for their participation. At San Jose, students are allowed to take a maximum of six special studies credits, which limits the use of a single student as a small group leader to one academic year. Funds are not available to provide the course with regular teaching assistants.

Although filmstrips are not commonly used in higher education, the decision to use this equipment rather than slide projectors was both instructionally and fiscally sound.

- Filmstrip projectors are easy to use, contain their own projection screen, and are substantially less expensive than slide projectors ($85 versus $150 or more per station). With slide projectors, additional funds would be required for the purchase of rear projection screens and individual study carrels. In this facility a number of filmstrip viewers are placed on standard tables for the students to use.
- Filmstrips at 3 cents per frame are far less expensive than 35-mm slides (20 cents or more each).
- A filmstrip projector requires approximately 50 percent of the power needed by a 35-mm slide projector and less room, reducing significantly the costs of both installing and operating the facility.

A comprehensive student manual was also developed to provide the students with guiding questions on their weekly reading assignments and follow-up materials on the learning laboratory exercises.

Results. The project has been successful. Learning has increased, students' attitudes toward both art and the course are more positive, and a number of graduate students are improving their teaching skills and enjoying the experience. The instructor's attitude toward the course has become enthusiastic as the quality of the course has improved, and her contact with individual students has increased. The new format not only provided the students with an opportunity to ask questions but, by using the self-paced approach, allowed them more time for taking notes and for studying the material. In addition, by using this pattern of instruction, the students' active involvement was increased, and the course has been able to reach a larger number of students without an increase in staffing. This project is also a fine example of how a number of media (film, filmstrips, and audio cassettes), when selected with care, can be used effectively within a single course to improve the quality, effectiveness, and efficiency of instruction.

Future Directions. Recognizing the continuing development of new instructional technologies such as interactive video disc, CDROM (Compact Disc Read Only Memory), and other computer-assisted instruction systems that provide an increased capability for random access to sight and sound, the staff involved with this project are exploring their applications to various aspects of this course. For example, video discs from the National Gallery of Art are being used, on an experimental basis, in the small group sessions to promote discussions. Plans are in place to investigate the applications of other technologies as their use becomes fiscally feasible.

Information Source on Technology in Education

For the latest information on research dealing with the use of instructional media and of new developments in the area, contact the Educational Resources Information Center (ERIC) Clearinghouse on Information Resources (School of Education, Syracuse University, Syracuse, New York 13244). This federally funded agency has been established specifically for this purpose.

Evaluating Existing Materials

Using commercially available materials almost always costs less, both in time and money, than designing and producing new ones. This is particularly true of computer-based units, film, and TV. The available media (print and nonprint) selected for use, however, should meet several specific criteria.

1. The instructional objectives of your unit and of the materials must agree.

2. The media should be appropriate for the instructional method selected.
3. The time required to go through the instructional materials must be within the range allocated.
4. The materials must be designed for your specific student population.

Make sure the instructional materials meet the established needs, rather than modifying your goals and objectives so that something now on the market can be used.

Selecting Materials

Selecting materials involves two phases: first, locating those materials that might be useful and, second, evaluating the materials themselves. Many basic references can help locate materials quickly. Most computer stores offer a wide selection of software and provide preview opportunities. In addition, ads for software and related evaluations can often be found in media or discipline-related professional journals. Most college and university audiovisual centers also have a collection of the numerous company and film library catalogues. Of course, the faculty themselves are often an excellent source of information about existing resources.

Once the specific items are located, the evaluation process begins in earnest, and at this phase many problems occur. Unfortunately, most of these problems exist because many publishers fail to provide information that faculty have been requesting for years: statements concerning the target population, prerequisites, objectives, testing data, and so on. Although some publishers do provide this data, most do not, so each faculty member or team considering the potential use of the item has to repeat a detailed analysis of it.

Most materials are eliminated quickly on the basis of wrong format, wrong content, or poor quality. One very useful technique has been to look at the separate parts of the materials rather than at the whole package. For example, commercially available slide series, filmstrips, computer software (courseware) packages, and programmed booklets can be purchased, broken up into separate sequences, and used very effectively for remedial work and review. A few sequences divided in this manner can easily serve large numbers of students when the sequences are placed in an independent learning laboratory or on reserve in the library.

It may seem uneconomical to break up a book by using only one or a few of its chapters. Not so! Most instructors find a book in which only a part is ideally suited for the course. On the one hand, asking students to buy the whole book in order to use just a few chapters may alienate them, and duplicating a chapter or so and then distributing it to the class raises copyright questions. On the other hand, trying to cover the material in a class setting usually wastes crucial instructional time. In these instances, why not purchase multiple copies, bind the sections needed separately, and place them in reserve in the library or laboratory, or write the publisher for permission to duplicate? Even if a modest fee is charged, this approach is cost effective.

There are specific advantages in placing copies of chapters or computer programs in an independent learning laboratory or on reserve in the library.

1. With books, each chapter or segment may be read individually, increasing the number of students who have access to materials from the same chapter at the same time.
2. Introductory and follow-up materials may be added to guide the student through the assignment, and "self-evaluation" quizzes may also be incorporated. Additional instructions are often required with many computer programs where excellent "software" is supported in many instances with extremely poor directions.
3. The cost to the student of books and other instructional materials can be substantially reduced.

Segments from purchased tapes, filmstrips, and films also can be extremely useful. The decision to purchase should depend on the relationship between use, the number of sets required, and the quantity of the original items that will be used.

Design and Field Testing of Materials

Obviously, if existing materials are not usable, new units must be designed, produced, and evaluated. Once again the specific format and approach selected should be the ones that are the easiest to use within the constraints of time and budget. The emphasis should be on the instructional goals rather than using a specific approach or equipment system. The large number of language laboratories and television systems that can be found in storage on many campuses is mute testimony to instances, as noted earlier, in which the glamour of the hardware systems overshadowed a rational basis for their purchase and use.

While we are not covering the selection and design of media in detail, certain design steps should be followed.

1. State the objectives (available from earlier planning).
2. Design related criterion tests (produced from the objectives).
3. Review all anticipated student prerequisites. (What assumptions are made about entering student competencies, and are they accurate?)
4. Select the instructional format.
5. Design a preliminary draft (or an experimental edition) of the sequence.
6. Field test the preliminary draft (still in rough format) on several students who meet the definition of the population.
7. Revise the preliminary draft. (Field testing often will identify specific differences between actual and anticipated prerequisites.)
8. Continue the testing on small populations and revise as necessary.
9. Produce a final field test edition for a pilot study or field test program.

To assist in this process, a short questionnaire called the MINI-QUEST has proven to be useful in evaluating a single unit, lesson, or sequence (Exhibit 3).

It is surprising how much useful data can be obtained

Exhibit 3. MINI-QUEST Questionnaire for Evaluation of Materials.

Student Evaluation of Materials

Date _____ Material Title _____

Course Title _____ Instructor _____

Please circle the most appropriate alternative.

1. INTEREST
   These materials were:
   (1) very uninteresting
   (2) uninteresting
   (3) interesting
   (4) very interesting

2. PACE
   These materials were:
   (1) much too fast
   (2) a little too fast
   (3) just right
   (4) a little too slow
   (5) much too slow

3. LEARNED
   I learned:
   (1) nothing
   (2) very little
   (3) a fair amount
   (4) a great deal

4. CLARITY
   These materials were:
   (1) very unclear
   (2) unclear
   (3) clear
   (4) very clear

5. IMPORTANCE
   What I learned was:
   (1) very unimportant
   (2) unimportant
   (3) important
   (4) very important

6. GENERAL
   Generally, these materials were:
   (1) poor
   (2) fair
   (3) good
   (4) excellent

7. Please indicate any questions raised by these materials.

8. Please write at least one specific comment here about the materials. (Use the back if necessary.)

Thank you!

---

from such a simple instrument. Such data tell immediately if the unit was interesting, clear, paced properly, and generally effective. Student answers to the open-ended question also prove to be invaluable.

Careful pilot testing on representative students at this point will substantially reduce the problems that may occur when the materials are used as part of the formal program. There are some excellent references available in the selection, use, and production of instructional materials that can prove extremely helpful. These include

Harnafin, M. J., and Peck, K. L. *The Design, Development, and Evaluation of Instructional Software.* New York: Macmillan, 1988. (An additional source of information that focuses on computer-assisted instruction.)

Heinich, R., Molenda, M., and Russell, J. D. *Instructional Media and the New Technologies of Instruction.* New York: Macmillan, 1986.

Kemp, J. E. *The Instructional Design Process.* New York: Harper & Row, 1985.

Kemp, J. E., and Dayton, D. K. *Planning and Producing Instructional Media.* (5th ed.) New York: Harper & Row, 1980.

Locatis, C. N., and Atkinson, F. D. *Media and Technology for Education and Training.* Westerville, Ohio: Merrill, 1984.

Materials for Visual Presentations—Planning and Preparation, a series of pamphlets available through the Motion Picture and Audiovisual Markets Division of Eastman Kodak, Rochester, New York.

Logistical Coordination

New programs, whether they cover a single course or only a three-week instructional sequence implemented as a pilot project, can be extremely complex, especially if an attempt has been made to individualize the program and to combine independent study with traditional group sessions. The scope and nature of these individualized programs make it extremely important that all of the elements be carefully coordinated and that materials be available in sufficient quantity at the right time and in the right place.

Although logistical coordination is an obvious need, it is often overlooked. The reason for this oversight is perhaps a human one: most of us are not interested in the step-by-step analyses and preparation required to make sure that all the elements are ready and available.

For example, on one campus a very successful program was expanded from approximately 100 students to 300. In planning for this increase, the staff considered the number of classrooms required but completely overlooked the need to increase the independent learning units, an integral part of the course. As a result, when the semester began, the number of sets of material on reserve in the library was not increased sufficiently, and many students found it impossible to get through the units in the required time. The result was chaos, confusion, and loss of tempers—an excellent program was damaged by careless management.

In a course on another campus, the same type of problem occurred when the faculty and support staff who had carefully designed the instructional elements, new materials, and testing procedures overlooked the essential student orientation session for the new program. In this instance, two weeks were lost when puzzled students tried to understand what they were to do and where they were to do it. Orientation is extremely crucial when the program represents a departure from tradition. Do not expect students to trust a statement of objectives when for years they have reported that faculty say one thing, teach another, and test for a third.

The logistical problems vary from project to project. Generally, however, they cover the following areas.

1. *Classroom availability:* The required number of rooms should be scheduled, and the assigned rooms must meet size and media requirements. (This is particularly important in programs that utilize various types of structures in a flexible pattern.)
2. *A student communications system:* In larger classes procedures must be established to ensure that important information, such as scheduling changes and additional class meetings, reach the students. These procedures are very important when a regular class pattern is not being followed.
3. *A functioning support system:* Be sure that the logistical support areas (library, independent learning laboratory, and so on) are ready and able to handle the students when they arrive. Can tests and other evaluation and diagnostic instruments be scored and interpreted in the available time? Are the most efficient methods of tabulation being used, and are

the procedures established to collect all the evaluation data that are required?

4. *Proper numbers of materials to meet program needs:* This is particularly important if independent study is involved. The exact number of units that will be required is affected by the length of the sequence, the number of students, the number of concurrent assignments, how much time the students have between the initial assignment and its completion, the particular study pattern of the students, and various external elements, such as vacation periods and assignments in other courses. The best advice is to have more sets of materials or work stations than you anticipate and then base future decisions on the data that are collected regarding use.

Usually the ratio of sets of material to students falls between 1:10 and 1:20. Experience has shown, however, that patterns of use vary substantially from course to course and, in fact, may change in a single program from one semester to the next. This is particularly true as students adjust their study patterns according to experience. For example, in an individualized biology laboratory, students tended at first to wait until the end of the week before going to the laboratory and, as a result, found themselves waiting in long lines. Within a few weeks, however, the pattern had changed, and most students completed their assignments earlier, thus improving the efficiency of the operation.

New course patterns and procedures are often difficult for a student to understand as they are encountered for the first time. A student manual can play a vital role in the success of a new program that breaks from the more traditional approach. The design and use of a manual are described in detail in the next chapter.

At the completion of this step, all materials have been produced and field tested. The course is designed and ready for full implementation and field testing. Now the design group will find out whether their efforts have been successful.

9

Preparing
a Descriptive Manual
for Students

In this chapter, we will discuss the need for and use of a student manual: what should be included and possible resources to aid in its production. A copyright agreement is also discussed.

Overview

- "The manual provides a succinct presentation of relevant course materials, which helps the student to define what is important for this particular course."
- "It helped a great deal. Faculty colleagues from other institutions have been able to easily adapt and adopt the course with limited guidance from me. In addition, I have very few requests for clarification of course requirements, time lines, grading criteria or standards, or weekly assignments. Perhaps some faculty look forward to such repeated discussions — I prefer to teach."
- "A terrific idea. The students can refer to it [the manual] throughout the semester, and they considered it to be one of the most positive aspects of the course."
- "The greatest advantage for me is that it enables me to get a

157

variety of materials in students' hands efficiently and effectively."

- "The manual provided necessary coherence for the class. Without it, the course would not only have appeared 'experimental' but unorganized or even incoherent. The manual provided important information and semblance of rationality. It gave all of us a common plan and reference."

Faculty often invest a great deal of time in improving the content and structure of courses, the quality of the materials they use, and the equity of their examinations. Despite these efforts, many spend countless hours with individual students reviewing content, attempting to clarify assignments, and generally helping their students (and perhaps themselves) to survive their courses.

While many of the instructional problems faced by faculty are to be expected, others are unnecessary. Instances in which students do not understand their assignments, they study the wrong content for a test, or there is confusion as to how grades will be determined must be avoided. In a review of the problems faced by students, a course approval committee at the University of Maryland (Rubin, 1985) identified a series of important questions that were repeatedly not answered in the syllabi provided by the faculty to their students.

- Why would a student want to take this course?
- What are the course objectives? Where do they lead, intellectually and practically?
- What are the prerequisites? What does the faculty member assume that the students already know? Will the necessary missing skills be taught during the course?
- Why do the parts of the course come in the order they do?
- Will the course be primarily lecture, discussions, or group work?
- What does the professor expect from the students?
- What is the purpose of the assignments?
- What will the tests test? memory? understanding? ability to

synthesize, to present evidence logically, to apply knowledge in a new context?

- Why have the books been chosen? What is their relative importance in the course and in the discipline?

An effectively used and carefully designed student manual (our term for a more comprehensive syllabus) can improve the learning that takes place by helping to answer these and other questions, and it can improve communication, significantly reducing problems for both faculty and student.

Just as courses differ, no two manuals should be alike. The final decision about the form and content of a student manual must be based on the actual structure of the course, the number of students involved, the type of course (lecture, laboratory, field experience, discussion, and so on), the learning goals, what students are expected to do, and how much direction the faculty wishes the students to have.

A well-designed student manual also tells the students that the faculty are as interested in helping them to succeed as in the content of the course.

Why Use a Student Manual?

A student manual serves a wide variety of functions, all designed to make the role of faculty easier and the students' roles and responsibilities clearer.

- A manual defines student responsibilities for successful completion of the course. One of the biggest problems students have is managing time effectively. If the students have a clear idea of what they are expected to accomplish and a time frame for completion, they are more likely to finish assignments on time and be appropriately prepared for exams.
- A manual can improve the efficiency of student note taking and studying. Students' class time is frequently spent copying detailed formulas and diagrams or attempting to distinguish important from unimportant information. Stu-

dents may miss the major points of the presentation. A manual can include outlines of information to be covered, reproduction of essential diagrams and tables, and copies of the overhead transparencies used to enhance discussion. In this way the contents of the manual organize and focus student note taking and studying.

- A manual can reduce test anxiety. Providing students with sample questions in a manual has a positive impact on learning while significantly reducing test anxiety. The more students know about the instructional priorities, the more effective and efficient they can be in their studying.
- A manual acquaints learners with the logistics of the course. Many courses vary significantly in terms of the days classes are held, the instructors for each class, and the type of sessions that occur (that is, guest lecturers, simulations, films, and so on). A manual details this information so that students know what to expect at each class meeting.
- A manual can provide a compendium of readings that are difficult to obtain. There are times when courses are developed before comprehensive literature is available on the topic. The manual can include copies of articles the faculty want the students to read. (If a manual is used in this way, be certain that the necessary copyright clearances are obtained.)
- A manual can include handouts that might otherwise have been distributed individually. Faculty frequently distribute handouts as they become appropriate to the topics covered. If these handouts are included in a manual, students find it easier to keep all the course information together and accessible. Materials of this type often include tables, charts, graphs, and diagrams that, while important, are not found in the required texts.

Getting a Manual Typed, Printed, and Distributed

A comprehensive student manual can run anywhere from twenty to well over a hundred pages. Therefore, before work begins on putting a manual together, a process that can take a great deal of time and effort, the basic logistics of production and distribution should be addressed.

If the number of students is over 100 or so each semester, there are publishers who not only will print and distribute the manuals but will, as part of their service, also take care of obtaining the necessary clearances from other publishers and authors. They may also pay royalties. Faculty who go this route should make sure that royalties are paid each semester rather than at the time when all printed manuals are sold. Also, build in the necessary number of free desk copies. At Syracuse, faculty supported in the development of the manuals by the university share these royalties with the institution. In addition, care must be taken to obtain the necessary permission to reprint articles that are to be included. Some publishers will, as noted earlier, take care of this extremely time-consuming and sometimes costly process. There are, in addition, a growing number of smaller printing/duplication stores located near college campuses that will both print and sell such manuals. These stores copy directly from the faculty's materials and do not generally provide editorial or graphic assistance. Such publishers include:

Copley Publishing Group
256 Great Road
Littleton, MA 01460-1918

Ginn Press
191 Spring Street
Lexington, MA 02173-8087

Kendall/Hunt Publishing Company
2460 Kerper Boulevard
Dubuque, IA 52001

Is Support Available? While some institutions have staff available who will help in typing, graphics, and editing, others do not. The faculty member writing the manual must find out what resources are available to assist in the production of the manual. Is there a Center for Instructional or Faculty Development with staff who can help in typing and editing? What kind of help can a faculty member get from his or her department?

Many chairpersons or deans can provide typing assistance and make available some salary dollars in the summer to assist faculty during this heavy writing period. In other instances, summer stipends come directly from the central administration. On some projects, a portion of this money is used to provide the help of a graduate assistant. If graphics support is needed, it is usually available through a media or audiovisual center.

Production. Most academic departments have funds set aside to cover the printing costs of classroom handouts and short syllabi. However, these monies usually are not adequate to support the free distribution of more complete student manuals which may, depending on the quantity being printed and the number of pages, cost well over $1,000 to print for a class of several hundred students. For this reason we recommend selling these manuals to the students through the college bookstore, other normal textbook channels, or local duplicating stores that provide these services.

The advantages of selling these manuals through one of these outlets are many:

1. There is no fiscal risk to the faculty or to the academic department.
2. Some bookstores, as well as duplicating stores, are willing to handle the printing as well, significantly reducing the faculty member's production concerns.
3. It is possible to build in royalties for the authors or, if fiscal support has been given, to the department or institution.
4. If the quality is high, students accept paying for the manuals as they would for any other course-related resource.

As a rule of thumb, we find the selling price of a manual produced within the institution determined in the following manner.

*   50 percent production cost
*   15 percent royalties

- 10 percent desk copies and overruns
- 25 percent bookstore markup

Royalties and Copyright

As noted previously, writing a quality student manual takes time and effort, time that the writer(s) could be devoting to research, to other writing, or to other financially rewarding activities. Paying royalties on the sale of these manuals recognizes the worth of the effort and, in one small way, helps to balance the reward system between teaching, research, and publication.

Since a manual may contain significant new material, some consideration should be given to copyrighting it. At Syracuse, where most manuals are produced with the assistance of the Center for Instructional Development, a formal royalty and copyright policy is in place. If sales are anticipated outside of the institution or if significant new material is contained in the manual, copyright will be held by the university. If this is not the case and the manual is limited in use to a specific course, the author(s) may apply for copyright. A copy of the Syracuse University Publication Agreement, when copyright is held by the institution, may be found in Resource A.

What to Include

There are an infinite number of ways to design a student manual. What follows is a description of the sections that might be included. However, as mentioned previously, ultimately the content and form are completely up to the faculty and will depend upon the nature of the students and the type of course that is being offered.

In deciding what the manual will contain, those developing it should keep in mind that the overall purpose of a student manual is to

- Describe the course, its goals, and its objectives
- Describe the structure of the program (particularly any nontraditional aspects of it that may be new to the students)

- Acquaint the students with their responsibilities for the course
- Provide critical logistical and procedural information about what will happen and where

The manual should not be considered a replacement for a "live" orientation. Rather it is structured to supplement the orientation in meeting the practical needs of the students by answering the operational questions they may have as the course progresses.

The content of the manual varies from course to course, as does its general format. However, the following items are usually required for an effective student manual. (Note: the specific order in which these items are covered is not absolute.)

1. Title and number of the course
2. Letter to the student expressing the intent of the course in its present form, and if the program is experimental, asking cooperation in the extensive evaluation that will take place
3. Table of contents
4. Purpose of the manual and how to use it
5. Introduction
   - Status of course (that is, pilot, experimental)
   - Rationale (how this course fits into the general program and for whom it was designed)
   - Any general directions for the student
   - Where notices and grades, and so on, will be posted
6. Personnel involved in the course and how to contact them (office hours, phone, and so on). Those involved in the design of the course might also be listed. If the manual is to be used over several semesters, the names of the personnel should be omitted or the manual should be designed so the student can complete this information on the first day of class.
7. Overview of content
   - Instructional flow diagram (introduction)
   - Course outline

- Module outline (may come later in explanation of each module)
- Options explained
- General course objectives

8. Evaluation and/or grading procedures
   - Credits and grades explained
   - Requirements/assignments
   - Scales or forms that will be used
9. Logistical forms
   - To request and/or change options
   - To notify faculty of problems and errors in the materials
10. Specifics of each unit
    - Objectives, options, projects, grades, place, time, personnel, flow diagram, requirements/assignments
11. Materials
    - Texts, and so on; where and how to get them and how to use them
    - Manual may include some materials such as bibliographies, charts, and so on
12. Calendar
    - Places and times for units, projects, meetings, minicourses, deadlines, and so on (often the calendar can be combined effectively with the flow diagram for each module). Again, if the manual is to be used over several semesters, specific dates should be omitted.
13. Facilities
    - Where they are and how to use them—that is, learning laboratory, library, museum, and so on
14. Checklist
    - List of all things to be done is put in one place for the student to refer to quickly
15. Self-tests (with answers)
    - Designed to give the students an opportunity to see if they can meet the stated objectives
16. Copyright or credit notices
17. (Optional) Readings or other materials (such as forms to be turned in) that are necessary and not available elsewhere. Also included in this section may be copies of

complex diagrams or other visuals that will be used by the faculty member during lectures, chronologies, and materials on using the library or computing center.

Since the manual will be used by students, it should be written to students—using the familiar "you" whenever possible. It should be clear and precise. This becomes especially important as the programs grow more complex in their structure. Of particular importance are the flow diagrams which, if used well and designed with care, can be very effective in communicating the scope of the program and extensive logistical information. If complex drawings are to be used in large lecture sections, reduced copies should be included in the manual. Also effective is leaving space for taking notes if the manual is to be referred to during the lecture. The following guide to writing student manuals includes representative pages from a number of manuals in various disciplines and has been found to be most useful:

Rodgers, C. A., and Burnett, R. E. *Student Manuals: The Rationale and Design.* (Rev. ed.) Syracuse, N.Y.: Center for Instructional Development, Syracuse University, 1981.

Reducing the Cost

Printing small quantities of materials is expensive and, although the students will usually purchase the manual (since note taking in the manual is encouraged), attempts should be made to keep the cost to a minimum. One way of substantially lowering the cost of a manual is by either separating the "unique" semester information (calendar, faculty, office hours, specific options, and so on) from the main body of the material and giving it to the students separately as a handout or leaving space for them to fill in this information. While this is possible only after a course is stabilized, it can reduce the cost significantly by allowing more copies of the manual to be printed at one time for use during several semesters. A well-designed student manual can improve the effectiveness of the course and reduce significantly the frustration caused by poor communication between faculty and students.

10

Implementing, Evaluating, and Refining the Course or Program

◆

This chapter focuses on the role of evaluation during implementation and revision. Three detailed case studies are presented to show how data can be collected and used.

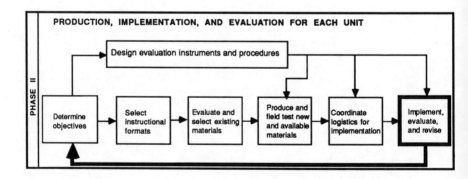

PHASE II

PRODUCTION, IMPLEMENTATION, AND EVALUATION FOR EACH UNIT

Design evaluation instruments and procedures

| Determine objectives | Select instructional formats | Evaluate and select existing materials | Produce and field test new and available materials | Coordinate logistics for implementation | Implement, evaluate, and revise |

Overview

At this point in the development process the complete body of instruction is tested operationally. This may be done by conducting a pilot study for a single unit of the course or for the entire program, using a limited number of students. While it is sometimes impossible to avoid, it is unwise to involve a large number of students (several hundred) in the initial trial of a new program. Large numbers of students limit the ability to find rapid solutions to some problems that may occur. With smaller numbers, design deficiencies can be corrected as they are identified, significantly reducing student and faculty frustration.

During this step, data are collected to determine how well the program objectives—both the overall and the unit-by-unit objectives—are being met. Based on this information revisions are then made in format and materials. Every project can be expected to go through several design/field test/revision sequences before it can be considered fully operational. As problems in the program are identified and solved, it is possible to increase the number of students enrolled. Those responsible for the project should not begin by promising to accomplish too much in too short a time.

Improvement and modifications of the program can be expected to continue as students change, new faculty become involved, the content changes, and new methods become available. While far less comprehensive than the earlier efforts, a modest evaluation effort should be continued. The evaluation and redesign of the introductory psychology course at Syracuse University show how the course evolves through such a process.

Case Study: Introductory Psychology

In the fall of 1983, the psychology department at Syracuse University, building upon an earlier project in the department, introduced a new first-year course that was designed to provide all students with the same basic program. Previously, individual sections had been taught by different faculty using textbooks supporting his or her own approach to psychology. As a result, the faculty teaching the courses that followed could make few if any assumptions about what the students already knew, a problem that was causing major problems in the department.

Recognizing the potential problems associated with having several faculty and nearly a dozen graduate students offering a single course to approximately 800 students, the department asked the Center for Instructional Development to formally evaluate the new program and to make recommendations based on the findings. An evaluation protocol was cooperatively developed and administered, and student performances on tests and examinations were analyzed.

To collect these data, several steps were taken. Staff attended lectures, a random number of recitation sections, and meetings of faculty involved with the course. Interviews were conducted with the recitation leaders (graduate students), the large group lecturers, other faculty, the department chair, and the course coordinator. The students were surveyed in the middle and at the end of the course.

While the course generally ran smoothly for a first offering of this type, several specific problems were identified.

- The course, while crucial to the department, was perceived by many as not covering the content considered essential.
- The lectures (divided among four different faculty) were uneven in quality and preparation and lacked continuity.
- The room in which the lectures were held was poorly suited to the use of the visuals (vital to the course) and had an inadequate sound system.
- Reading assignments among the four lecturers were uneven in terms of both length and difficulty.
- There was too much emphasis on "word lists" and definitions and too little emphasis on important concepts.
- The role of the course coordinator was not clear.
- Quizzes and examinations were based primarily on textbook materials and did not include questions related to the lecture topics or the recitation discussions; consequently, lectures and recitations were perceived by students as unimportant.

- There was some disagreement as to the exact role of the recitation leaders.

To address these concerns, a number of actions were taken.

1. The location of the lectures was moved.
2. To provide greater continuity, the department made efforts to reduce the number of new lecturers from semester to semester and to improve the quality of materials that were used. Greater effort was also taken to ensure that the content of the lectures meshed with the specific goals of the course.
3. A comprehensive student manual was produced. This manual, in addition to describing the general operation of the course and the role of each component, spelled out grading procedures and instructional objectives and provided representative questions and vocabulary lists. The manual also provided content guidelines to faculty responsible for the large lectures. In the latest version, selected readings have also been added.
4. Quizzes and examinations were restructured to be more comprehensive, stressing the major objectives of the course, and to include elements covered in both lectures and recitations as well as in the text. Scored items were analyzed, and poorer items were replaced or rewritten.

Results have been very positive. The ratings of the lectures have improved significantly; students have found grading to be fairer and exams to better indicate knowledge and relate more to course work. In addition and perhaps most significant, enrollment has increased from 800 to 1300 students.

In addition, the student manuals were rated extremely high as to usefulness and clarity. The fall 1984 student survey showed, with the improvement of the lectures, increased concern about the recitation session on the part of the students. Improvements in the recitation section were made during the following year, and a major revision of the entire course is now under way to meet the needs generated by a significant increase in student enrollment. The following comment from the course coordinator best describes the success of this project. "During the current fall semester, attendance at the lectures runs about 90 to 95 percent (up from about 50 percent in its first year). In addition, there is close cooperation and weekly meetings among the TAs [teaching assistants] and lecturers. Although a fair amount of experience with this format would inevitably tend to improvement, the contributions by CID [Center for Instructional Development], I feel, in terms of diagnoses of problems and specific recommendations, were invaluable in the speed with which the course has improved and reached this status. I also found the data extremely valuable as I trained new teaching assistants entering the program."

Formative evaluation also played an important role in refining the successful music course described in the following case study.

Case Study: Music for the Nonmusic Major

On the next few pages, you will find two operational outlines of the first four-week module of a music course for the nonmusic major designed at the State University College, Fredonia, New York. The first diagram, Figure 26, shows what the project looked like during its first field test; the second, Figure 27, shows the same segment modified for use the following semester after the initial field testing and evaluation were completed. (A detailed report on this study, An Individual Approach to Music for the Non-Music Major, #7, by Robert M. Diamond, Thomas Regelski, and Donald Lehr, has been published by the Instructional Resources Center, State University, Fredonia, New York, June 1971.) (Note: Although this project was completed some time ago, the process that was used in its development is almost identical to the one now used at Syracuse.)

The introductory module was designed to provide each student with an orientation to and framework for the entire course and with the prerequisites that were necessary for the units that follow. Since the student population was extremely diverse—some students had had as many as eight years of formal music training while others had none — three tracks were used, with assignments based on the performance of the students on the pretest. Level I students had the most comprehensive music background; Level II students had some musical experience or course work; and students assigned to Level III had little, if any, related skills.

The changes that were made as a result of the field test and the reasons for them are as follows (notice how these changes affected the operational sequence).

1. The course overview and the pretest were separated to improve the orientation session. *Rationale:* The course was such a major departure from the more traditional courses with its emphasis on independent study and student options that many students found the transition to it extremely difficult. It also became obvious that additional time had to be spent reviewing how to use the student manual effectively as well as explaining how the statements of instructional objectives could be used to improve learning while increasing the effectiveness of study time.

2. The sequencing of seminars within the module had to be substantially changed. *Rationale:* For an effective seminar to take place, a certain amount of background information is essential. The original sequence did not provide students with enough study time to complete the necessary units before they were discussed. The seminars therefore were rescheduled later in the module.

3. New instructional units were required. *Rationale:* On the posttest, students did not perform at the anticipated level in their ability either to read scores or to discriminate aurally. Two additional independent study units, a tape/slide sequence on score reading and a programmed booklet with audio, were added. As a result, students' deficiencies were corrected.

4. One unit had to be completely redesigned. *Rationale:* The multiscreen presentation on style proved to be instructionally ineffective and disliked (an understatement) by the students. This approach also proved cumbersome and inef-

Figure 26. Music in the Western World: Instructional Module.

Fall Field Test Version

INTRODUCTION
AND
PREREQUISITES

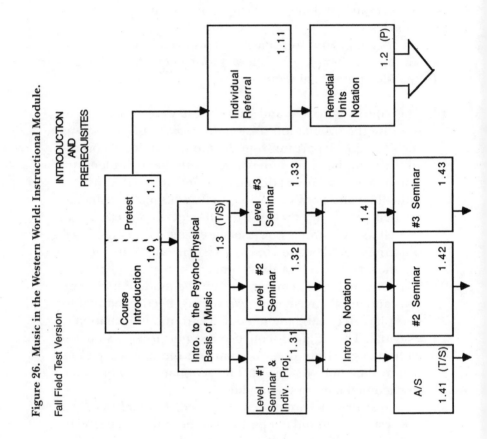

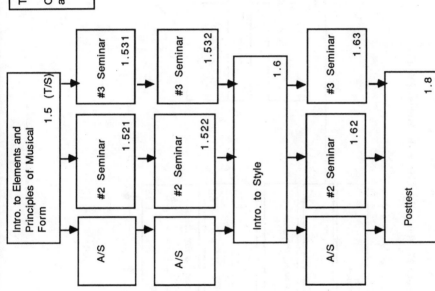

Twice Weekly

Optional Listening
and Review Sessions
1.7

KEY: A/S = As assigned by instructor
P = Programmed Booklet
T/S = Tape/Slide

Intro. to Elements and
Principles of Musical
Form   1.5 (T/S)

A/S

A/S

#2 Seminar   1.521

#2 Seminar   1.522

#3 Seminar   1.531

#3 Seminar   1.532

Intro. to Style   1.6

A/S

#2 Seminar   1.62

#3 Seminar   1.63

Posttest   1.8

Source: Thomas Regelski, Robert M. Diamond.

Figure 27. Revised Music in the Western World.

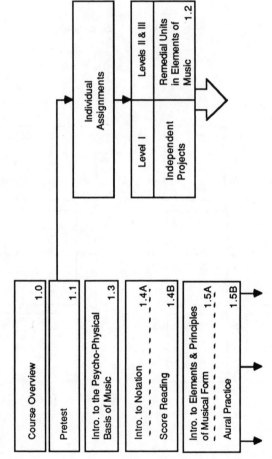

Spring Revision

Course Overview — 1.0

Pretest — 1.1

Intro. to the Psycho-Physical Basis of Music — 1.3

Intro. to Notation — 1.4A
Score Reading — 1.4B

Intro. to Elements & Principles of Musical Form — 1.5A
Aural Practice — 1.5B

Individual Assignments

Level I — Independent Projects

Levels II & III — Remedial Units in Elements of Music — 1.2

	Music in the Western World	
	Unit	Format
	1.0	Class
	1.1	Pretest
	1.2	P
	1.3	T/S
	1.4A	T/S
	1.4B	T/S
	1.5A	T/S
	1.5B	P/A
Level I	1.61-S	Seminar
Level II	1.62-S1	Seminar
"	1.62-S2	Seminar
Level III	1.63-S1	Seminar
"	1.63-S2	Seminar
"	1.63-S3	Seminar
	1.7	Text-T/S
	1.8	Posttest

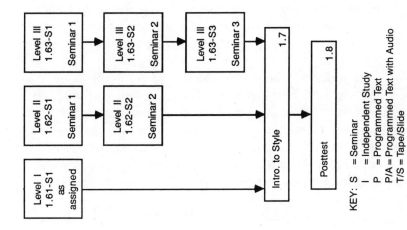

KEY: S = Seminar
       I = Independent Study
       P = Programmed Text
       P/A = Programmed Text with Audio
       T/S = Tape/Slide

Source: Thomas Regelski, Robert M. Diamond.

ficient as it forced all students to move at the same pace. It was replaced by a far more effective tape/slide sequence used in conjunction with written materials.

5. The number of seminars was reduced. *Rationale:* As sometimes happens, the fall and spring semesters did not have the same amount of time available for instruction, forcing a modification in design. By placing the seminars later in the sequence and scheduling more seminars for the Level III students and fewer for the well-prepared group, the number of seminars was reduced from fifteen to six. This decrease in the actual number of seminars did not appear to have a negative effect on either attitudes or achievement. In addition, to permit maximum flexibility, this three-hour course was scheduled for an hour a day (five hours each week) so that every student could attend any session scheduled during that period. Note, however, that the maximum number of live meetings a student would attend during the two-and-one-half-week module was six.

6. The twice-weekly optional listening and review sessions were replaced by optional audiotapes placed in the Independent Learning Laboratory. *Rationale:* Because of a heavy assignment load, students did not attend these regularly scheduled, optional, faculty-led review sessions.

In addition, minor modifications were made in the pretest, in some of the tape/slide sequences, and in the specific remedial units that were used. Several remedial assignments were also eliminated, and a more realistic time frame was established. It should also be noted that the effectiveness of the remedial module made it possible to eliminate the grouping by entering levels of proficiency once this unit was completed.

Keeping the Students Informed

There are times, particularly during the initial trial of a program, when it is essential that the students involved in the experimental or pilot group be kept informed of what is happening and what you are finding out through the evaluation process. Providing information to the students during this period serves several purposes. First, it gives the program credibility. Students know that you are listening to them and that you care. Second, as a result, they are willing to tolerate the intrusion of evaluation and, in fact, improve the quality of the information they provide; and third, if things do go wrong and problems occur, they tend to forgive and be far more positive to the whole experience than they might otherwise be. In one new project the students were willing to overlook an unrealistically heavy work load when they were informed that, as a result of their feedback, the assignments and time schedule were being changed for the next semester. A memorandum sent to students involved in the pilot run of the music course we have just described not only covered test results by level and described the student attitudes toward the test and individual units but also discussed the changes that were being made based on their input. Finally, the memorandum stressed how important the information they provided was to the development team and thanked them for their assistance.

The following case study of an economics course shows how faculty may use data collected to improve the effectiveness of instruction.

Case Study: Improving Teaching Effectiveness in Economics

Although the two previous case studies focused on collecting data for course improvement, sometimes questions are designed to collect data about teaching effectiveness. The use of data to improve teaching effectiveness is particularly helpful in multisection courses in which a number of teaching assistants or junior faculty teach various sections, laboratory, or discussion groups, usually coordinated or supervised by single senior faculty members.

In the micro- and macroeconomics courses discussed earlier, a single faculty member supervised more than a dozen teaching assistants responsible for approximately twenty sections of the course. To assist the supervising faculty member in this role and to provide information that could help these

Exhibit 4. Questionnaire for Small Group Discussion Leaders.

A one (1) represents *Not* at all, a three (3) represents *Somewhat*, and a five (5) represents *Very* much.

Please indicate the degree to which you perceive your instructor as:

	N	S		V
	N		S		V
• Prepared	1	2	3	4	5
• Organized	1	2	3	4	5
• Understandable in terms of level of presentation	1	2	3	4	5
• Understandable in terms of language	1	2	3	4	5
• Being open to questions	1	2	3	4	5
• Treating students with respect	1	2	3	4	5
• In control of the class	1	2	3	4	5
• Enthusiastic	1	2	3	4	5
• Answering questions effectively	1	2	3	4	5
• Caring about the subject	1	2	3	4	5
• Making students interested in the subject	1	2	3	4	5
• Providing high-quality instruction	1	2	3	4	5
• Motivating you to perform well in this course	1	2	3	4	5

beginning teachers improve their teaching, questions focusing specifically on their performance in the classroom were added to the end of the course questionnaire (Exhibit 4).

Other sections of the questionnaire dealt with such areas as course objectives, the student manual, the remedial mathematics sequences, course materials, the evaluation procedures, and instruments that were used and included a number of open-ended questions focusing on strengths and weaknesses of the course as students perceived them.

To make the teacher-focused questions particularly useful, the information collected was presented in three different ways. (See Exhibit 5.)

1.   The course coordinator received for *each* question an analysis of the data for every section. Since most teaching assistants were responsible for two sections, specific problem areas were easy to identify and counseling could begin.
2.   Each section leader was provided with a summary mean ranking of all sections that shows how they compared generally to the other section leaders.

Exhibit 5. Report to Individual Instructors — Selected Portion.

Item Mean Scores

Class/Section: ECN202 04
Overall Mean Score = 4.4
Rank over All Classes = 3 of 19

| | **Score** | | | |
Item/Question	This Class	All Classes	STD	N
• Instruction pace was about right.	3.7	3.6	0.9	31
• Required workload was about right.	4.0	3.6	0.8	31
• Degree exam questions were fair.	3.4	3.4	1.2	31
• Degree exam grading was fair.	3.5	3.6	1.0	31
• Degree exams covered what was taught.	3.9	3.7	1.1	31
• Degree exam time to finish was right.	2.5	3.7	1.3	31*
• Feedback was returned in timely manner.	3.5	3.7	1.0	31

* problem area

3. Each section leader also received his or her own summary for all items on the questionnaire.

Case Study: Orientation Program
for New Teaching Assistants

This project, undertaken at Syracuse University, represents an excellent example of the importance of collecting base data before a significant new program is implemented. The orientation program represented a major departure for the university in the way it trained and supported its teaching assistants and a major fiscal and resource commitment if it were to be continued after its pilot testing, so data collection was imperative to show the actual impact of the program on the participants and the institution.

To provide this information, a survey based on the earlier Diamond and Gray instrument was developed and administered to all teaching assistants at the university the semester before the new program was to get under way (Spring 1987). Focusing on their needs and the support they were receiving, this same instrument was administered again in the spring of 1988. By comparing the replies from first-year teaching assistants, it provided extremely useful data on how participants in the program were different from their counterparts from the year before.

In addition to interviewing the participants during the program and the experienced teaching assistants who were to serve as group leaders, the university collected data in a number of other ways. A mid-program and an end-of-program questionnaire were administered, deans and faculty supervising teaching assistants were interviewed during the fall semester following the program, and data on the effectiveness of the teaching assistants as teachers were collected in several large-enrollment courses.

The data collected proved invaluable in ensuring the continuation and institutionalization of the program and in identifying areas that needed improvement. While the first offering of the program was highly successful, there were areas in which change was necessary. The program that was offered in the summer of 1988 showed the effect of these data: more time was set aside for the students to find housing, international students who had studied previously in the United States could be excused from the international program, the amount of time spent in small groups was increased while the number of large group lectures was substantially reduced. The length of the program was also slightly reduced, and a number of other scheduling changes were instituted. The evaluation protocol was repeated once again to measure and identify the impact of these modifications.

It is anticipated that, while the scope and intensity of the evaluation effort will be reduced over time, there will always be an evaluation component in the program.

Summary

Data collection and its use are essential to the success of this model. Without planned information collection and evaluation, these three courses would not have reached the level of effectiveness that they have. Although some of the evaluation focuses on structure and role, other questions focus on the effectiveness of a single lesson or on the materials that are used or deal with the content and goals of the course. While a wide range of questions can be asked, there is neither enough time nor resources for the purpose. It is the responsibility of the design team to identify which information is most important to collect and which questions should be asked.

The course evaluation protocol in Resource D is designed to make this process less complicated and more efficient. The detail of the questions asked and the questions themselves will vary depending on the reason for the evaluation, the problems that are addressed, and the resources and time that are available for the evaluation itself. What is important is that key questions not be overlooked simply because no one thought of them at the time the evaluation was being designed.

11

Facilitating
Curriculum Improvement
Through a Central
Campus Agency

At Syracuse University, a uniquely potent
Center for Instructional Development spearheads
the campus-wide determination to find better ways
of teaching and learning. The center does not depend on elaborate "hardware" or massive funding.
It relies on the force of its ideas and on the willingness of the university to back them up [Gross, 1975].

Overview

Up to this point, we have been focusing on the process of
course and curriculum design, implementation, and evaluation.
Administrative support is an essential component of any change
effort, affecting how much instructional improvement can occur
and how rapidly positive changes can be implemented. The
administration is responsible for establishing a supportive climate and providing the resources that quality improvements
require.

Establishing an academic support unit on a campus can,
if it is properly administered, positively affect the instructional
program of that institution by providing several basic benefits:

First, it shows that the institution places a priority on teaching and learning. Second, it can improve significantly the effective use of existing resources. Third, it can improve the quality of learning, reduce attrition, and increase enrollment (at Syracuse, almost every course or program that has been developed with the Center for Instructional Development has shown an increase in enrollment). Fourth, it can reduce significantly the time required for new program implementation—unassisted faculty committees are often not very efficient, and the assistance of an outsider coordinating and facilitating the process has significantly reduced the time needed for designing and implementing constructive change.

Three basic approaches are open to an institution interested in establishing a support agency—faculty development, instructional development, and organizational development. While overlap occurs, the focus of the agency determines the impact it has and how its success will be judged.

1. Faculty development focuses primarily on the individual faculty member—common activities include classroom visits by professional staff, workshops on teaching and evaluation, personal counseling, and the use of video to analyze teaching styles and techniques.
   Major outcomes of faculty development:
   - Demonstrates institution's concern for the individual
   - Improves productivity of individual faculty members
   - Improves job satisfaction
   - Facilitates role change
   - Develops better teaching skills
2. Instructional development focuses primarily on the student, the course, or the curriculum—common activities include course and curriculum design, implementation, and evaluation.
   Major outcomes of instructional development:
   - Improves academic effectiveness and efficiency
   - Improves resource utilization
   - Improves learning

- Leads to increased enrollment and decreased attrition
- Increases faculty satisfaction with courses or programs

3. Organizational development focuses on the institution's structure and the relationship among its units—usually includes workshops, seminars, and individual consultation with administrators and faculty.

Major outcomes of organizational development:

- Clarifies relationships among units
- Diagnoses institutional problems
- Ensures communication and feedback
- Clarifies institutional or unit goals
- Facilitates program implementation
- Ensures that required support exists
- Improves institutional climate

Unlike faculty and instructional development, organizational development can be accomplished effectively by using an outside consultant who, given a specific task, comes to the college or university for a short period of time and then, when the task is completed, moves on.

Selecting the Instructional Development Option

After reviewing the range of options available, the decision at Syracuse University was to focus primarily on instructional development. This decision was based on several factors. First, instructional development is the broader of the three approaches and would therefore include elements of the other two within it. Second, it was felt that this approach would have far more impact on the students than the other options, given the limited resources. Faculty development, for example, is not only extremely time-consuming—an agency can spend as many as eighty-five man-hours assisting a single faculty member—but the effect is limited to having impact on those students enrolled in that particular faculty member's classes. Third, faculty development as it is usually implemented rarely questions "what is taught," focusing primarily on "how it is taught." What good is it to improve the effectiveness of a faculty member if what that person is teaching should not be taught in the first place? And fourth, instructional development can have a direct and positive impact on the faculty involved. Recently, a number of agencies such as the Instructional Development Program at the University of Rhode Island have begun to combine both faculty and instructional development activities. At Syracuse, where the main focus remains on course, program, and curriculum design and evaluation, the Center for Instructional Development has supported the efforts of the Senate Committee on Instruction in sponsoring faculty workshops on teaching and a number of microteaching and other faculty development activities. A recent publication by the center, *A Guide to Evaluating Teaching for Promotion and Tenure* (Centra, Froh, Gray, and Lambert, 1987), is an excellent example of such an activity.

As noted, instructional development can serve some of the more important functions associated with organizational development. For example, as a direct result of the center's activities, new support units have been established at Syracuse, and new flexible credit and continuous registration systems have been developed in cooperation with the registrar's office. The staff of the center have also played an active role in bringing offices and departments together as problems are identified and solutions found. It provides a case study that may be useful to others seeking to create a similar agency. Since this book has been built around the instructional model used at Syracuse, the choice is appropriate.

Case Study: The Center for Instructional Development (CID) at Syracuse University

- For the first time, we had a true open dialogue among colleagues. This would not have occurred without the involvement of CID.
- From working with CID, I gained incentive, encouragement, sanction, time, assistance, feedback, structure, and a schema for developing a course in an organized and thorough manner.
- We were hostile at first. I thought we were reinventing the

wheel. But the CID staff and process were so effective that they won me over wholeheartedly! I have seen the need for this component ever since.

- Academics generally interact poorly. CID's great strength is in fostering this interaction by continually forcing us to address the basic issues associated with teaching.
- The Center for Instructional Development is a unique resource at Syracuse University. While its like may exist on other campuses, its value—both proven and potential—is of particular significance at this juncture in the future of higher education.

Background

The creation of the Center for Instructional Development (CID) and the associated position of assistant vice-chancellor for instructional development was based on a series of assumptions.

1. The future of the institution rests on a high-quality and exciting academic program that will bring about increased student enrollment and decreased attrition.
2. Traditional curriculum and course structures are generally insensitive to the needs, interests, and abilities of the individual student, unaffected by the changing needs of society, and inefficient in their use of available talents and resources.
3. Major and long-lasting improvements in curriculum and instructional programming will not take place unless a stimulus for change is formally built into the institution.

The early 1970s were a period of major unrest on American campuses, and Syracuse was no exception. There is little doubt that the demands by students for the institution to pay greater attention to instruction also contributed to the decision to form this agency.

A 1975 publication, *Syracuse University's Center for Instructional Development: Its Role, Organization and Procedures* (Diamond,

1975), listed publicly the potential benefits the center might have if it were successful.

1. Improvement in learning
2. Improvement in student attitudes toward a course, toward a discipline, and toward the institution
3. Reduced attrition and increased enrollment
4. Increased efficiency and effectiveness in the role of the teacher, who will have greater opportunity for specialization as well as more time for seminars and individual contact with students
5. Increased flexibility in instructional design according to the needs, interests, and abilities of both the individual student and the faculty member (that is, when appropriate, instructional options will be available and diagnostic instruments will be used for identifying students' individual strengths and weaknesses so that they can be assigned to remedial units if necessary or given possible exemptions)
6. Improved utilization of instructional space
7. Increased flexibility in time required for an individual student to complete an instructional program
8. Greater sensitivity of the academic program to the needs of the community at large
9. Increased attention to teaching and instruction throughout the institution

Although a reduction in cost per student credit hour was not included among the primary objectives, it was anticipated that because of increased enrollment many redesigned courses would generate more student credit hours without any additional increase in instructional costs. In some instances savings could have resulted, but the principal intention of the center was to improve instructional quality by making maximum use of existing resources, not to reduce the costs of instruction.

Many of these same goals appeared as recommendations twelve years later in the report *Involvement in Learning: Realizing the Potential of American Higher Education,* published by the National Institute of Education in 1984.

Some Operational Guidelines

Any change agency that asks questions, tests assumptions, and collects data very likely could and would be perceived as a major threat by some faculty. In addition, an initial operational budget of under $150,000 for evaluation and development activities necessitates making maximum use of those resources that are available to it. To reduce the possible negative perception of the center and to increase productivity, several significant steps were taken.

- To reduce the impression that the center was an administrative arm of the university, the center was located outside of the administration building. An old house, previously used by a fraternity, fortunately became available and was modified to serve the needs of the unit. Paintings, sculptures, and plants were used to reduce the feeling of sterility and to provide a climate of warmth and support. While the center has recently moved into a new space, an effort has been made to maintain the supportive atmosphere of the original building.
- Staff of the center make it a practice to provide support to anyone asking for help—students, faculty, staff. While limited resources make it impossible to provide full support to every faculty member, most requests are met with some kind of assistance, even if it is only suggestions as to where to go for specific help or recommendations for specific steps they can take.
- The fact that the primary goal of the center is to help faculty get where they want to go is stressed repeatedly. The faculty are assured that the staff of the center understands that the faculty are the content experts and are responsible for the content decisions.
- The center does not start with a preconceived answer. Solutions are developed only after problems are identified and all alternatives are explored. Courses, programs, and materials developed as part of the center's activity fit no single mold and range from traditional to highly innovative.

- The center will work only with faculty willing to follow the center's procedures for developing course and curriculum design. Experience has shown that the systematic process that the center uses is efficient and that significant problems result when questions or steps are omitted.
- Priorities are necessarily placed on large projects that will affect greater numbers of students and faculty. Few projects are smaller than a course. Since the center's establishment, it has gradually moved toward focusing a greater percentage of its total activities on larger projects.
- The projects selected for development are provided with maximum support until they become fully operational.
- Since only stronger faculty are involved and successful projects tend to lead to faculty promotion, more than one faculty member is involved in any project, whenever possible, thus preparing for transition.
- Media are kept in perspective. A specific approach is selected only after a problem is identified and all options are explored. Technology is not always the answer. Changing the content and sequence of a course may not actually change how it is taught; lectures, discussion and the general time frame may remain as they were. As noted earlier, cost and effectiveness do not necessarily correlate.
- Available funds are used to support faculty summer employment rather than released time. Most of the activities associated with the design of a program can be accomplished during the academic year without requiring faculty released time or overload. Since meetings are usually held weekly or biweekly, the additional work load has not been excessive. During the production phase, however, when instructional materials, tests, and student manuals are being produced, extensive faculty time is essential, and this work ideally takes place during the summer. Furthermore, money invested in faculty for full-time employment during the summer (usually ranging from three to six weeks) generates far more productivity for the dollar than the same funds used for released time. Academic departments tend to give the faculty member on released time additional assignments and

to use some of this time for other purposes. At Syracuse, a discretionary fund of $12,000 to $15,000 for summer faculty salaries has not only proved adequate but also seems to represent the maximum number of major projects (five to seven) that can be effectively handled by the development staff. The center also covers, with few exceptions, the cost of producing and purchasing the instructional materials required for implementation.

Structure

To be effective, the agency established to support the improvement of instruction must be located relatively high in the administrative hierarchy of the institution. Ideally, the head of the agency should report *directly to the chief academic officer*. This location is essential for several reasons. It shows an institutional commitment to the agency, opens up channels of communication for the head of the unit to all academic and administrative offices at the institution, and permits the head of the agency to participate at key planning and organizational meetings. Locating such an agency within a single school or college can create major administrative problems and undermine the credibility of the unit.

The head of the agency should control the priorities of all functional units that provide services essential to its success. For example, most projects could not be implemented without the design of instructional materials and the production of printed materials (examinations, manuals, and so on). When a development agency cannot control all the various support functions it needs to succeed, frustrations, inefficiency, and failure result.

At Syracuse, this problem has been resolved by having the director of the center also hold the title of assistant vice-chancellor, to whom all the externally required support offices report (Figure 28).

While somewhat atypical, the graphics unit and an extremely important small, one-person printing unit have been located directly within the center. The graphics department does service the entire academic community, but an analysis of

Figure 28. Administration Organization:
Instructional Support Area, Syracuse University.

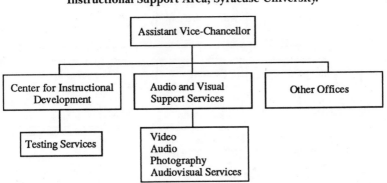

its activity showed that a large proportion of its daily work was devoted to center projects. Moving the audiovisual components out of the center also significantly reduced the erroneous perception on the part of some faculty that clients who came to the center for assistance would be "forced" to use media, a perception inherited from the practices of the unit the center replaced.

Another way of looking at components of a development agency is by function. To be effective, the development agency should contain or have direct access to the components shown in Figure 29. Also forming a part of CID is the Testing Services unit, which provides assistance to faculty in test construction and test scoring and analyses. This unit, which provides student rating data and other information used in the tenure and promotion process, has been clearly separated from CID. The center is solely a support agency. Only upon written request of a faculty member are CID data available for use in the promotion and tenure process.

Staffing

While most of the positions are traditional and need little introduction, two are unique to an instructional development agency and deserve attention.

The Instructional Developer. As noted earlier, the instruc-

Figure 29. Instructional Development Agency: Proposed Organization.

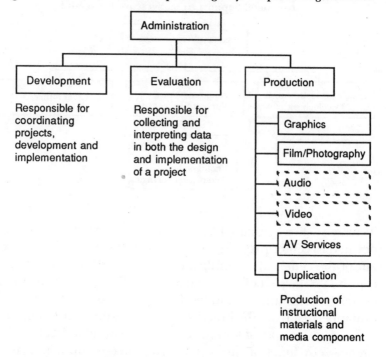

▰ ▰ ▰ ▰ UNITS NOT A FORMAL PART OF THE CENTER AT SYRACUSE, WITH SUPPORT AVAILABLE ON REQUEST.

tional developer is responsible for the overall design and implementation of each project. Chairing meetings, testing assumptions, and providing alternatives, the developer is the development agency's key staff member on any project. An effective developer combines efficient administrative skills with creativity and the ability to work well with people. Often placed in the role of editor, the developer also needs excellent writing skills. Unfortunately, a willingness to attend to details, creativity, and having excellent interpersonal skills are seldom found together. It is therefore more efficient to find individuals with these basic abilities who may have been outstanding teachers and to provide them with the expertise needed (instructional design theory, a sound base in use of terminology, evaluation, and so on) than it is to select individuals with the academic background and hope that these other traits will be developed on the job. An effective instructional developer also must be willing to let others (the faculty) own the successful projects with which he or she is involved. At times this can be a very difficult thing to do, but for the overall good of the project it is necessary.

Developers are demonstrably far more effective and efficient when they work outside their own disciplines. By coming from outside of the area, the developer is not perceived as a content threat by the faculty. The developer does not bring to the project the same vocabulary and assumptions as the faculty; and, more important, by being able to place himself or herself in the role of the student or as a result of being a noncontent expert, the developer is able to test assumptions, raise new alternatives, and question the status quo in a far less threatening way than would otherwise be possible.

As a rule of thumb, an effective developer can handle three to five major projects at a time, depending on their scope, the problems encountered, and the number and efficiency of faculty involved.

The Evaluator. Although an effective instructional developer must have some background in evaluation and have the ability to collect and interpret data, he or she, as well as the faculty, is too close to the project to view it objectively. On occasion specialized assistance and additional resources are needed to conduct the evaluation phase of a project. There are also many instances when the initial request from a school, department, or faculty member is for evaluation rather than design assistance, and staff must be available to meet this need.

While often missing, an evaluator within an instructional development agency can have a major impact on both the quality and success of the agency. Many projects begin long before an instructional developer is involved with a request by a department, school, or college for assistance in evaluating an ongoing program or in collecting needed data from employers, alumni, and so on.

It is extremely important that the evaluation staff of the unit be clearly separated from any office involved in collecting data for tenure and promotion purposes, however, because the design process must be open, honest, and supportive.

To perform successfully, the evaluator must be

- an effective communicator, able to interpret results verbally and in writing to those without a background in evaluation
- pragmatic — providing the information that is needed, when it is needed, and collecting it as efficiently as possible
- realistic — understanding that what may be fine for the laboratory is inappropriate and, in fact, often impossible in the instructional setting
- thoroughly familiar with all aspects of evaluation so that need determines approach rather than allowing approach to define the terms and scope of the evaluation

We have found, unfortunately, that the vast majority of individuals who are classified as evaluators do not have these competencies.

It is as difficult to find a good evaluator as it is to locate an effective instructional developer. While many calling themselves instructional developers focus more on product or on media, most evaluators tend to be narrow in scope and to place technique and design before need, and few are able to communicate what they have learned effectively to the rest of the world.

Without quality staff, an agency established to assist in improving academic programs cannot be successful.

Budget

The total number of dollars supporting a successful development effort may vary considerably from campus to campus. The larger the budget, the more projects that can realistically be undertaken at any one time. There is, however, a point at which the development staff could become too large, making quality control impossible — a point at which efficiency and effectiveness both suffer. In addition, the larger the budget of a support unit, the more vulnerable it becomes to cuts and outside pressures (a more detailed discussion follows in the section on agency survival). The more cost effective a unit is, the better its chance for survival; the larger a unit is, the more difficult for it to seem cost effective.

The base development and evaluation staff at Syracuse is extremely modest in size—one and one-half full-time professional developers (the director spends half his time in this function), one full-time professional evaluator, two to four doctoral interns in both evaluation and development, secretarial staff, and a one-person print shop. The number of full-time professional development and evaluation staff has increased from time to time with support provided by outside contracts and grants. The graphics staff, located in the center, and the testing services unit exist on most campuses and, although they are an integral part of the agency, should not be considered add-ons to support the mission of the center.

The budget of the center is primarily provided by the university. As a result, there are no charges to academic departments or faculty for services related to the improvement of instruction. There are, however, some charges associated with services provided to administrative departments and income-producing units or in the support of externally funded programs. The graphics, printing, and testing services units all produce income that offsets to a considerable degree their area budgets. The development and evaluation units become involved in externally funded projects only when the projects are compatible with the agency's mission to improve the quality of instruction and programs at the institution. It cannot afford to have its limited resources drained to serve offices and programs unrelated to the university.

For reference, a two-level budget follows (Table 4). Level I is a suggested start-up budget with the evaluation position, for example, filled on a part-time basis by an available faculty member. At this level, a number of services (graphics, media production, and so on) are provided by units that already exist on most campuses. Level II represents what might be considered, with the possible addition of one or two professional staff, several more graduate assistants, and one or two secretaries, a size of maximum efficiency. While traditional audiovisual sup-

Table 4. An Instructional Development Agency:
One Approach to Budgeting (Estimated)[a] — Add-On Positions Only.

	Level I (Minimum start-up)	Level II
Staff		
Director	$35,000[b]	$ 45,000[b]
Developer		30,000
Evaluator	15,000 (half-time)	30,000
Clerical/Administrative (3)	12,000	36,000
Graphic Artist	(available)	14,000
Graduate Assistants (4) (Development/Evaluation)		34,000[c]
Part-Time Help	3,000	4,000
Operating (Project Support)		
Office Supplies/Telephones	9,500	12,000
Travel	2,000	5,000
Instructional Materials (Commercial)	1,500	3,000
Graphic/Photo Supplies	2,500	3,000
Equipment	15,000[d]	30,000[e]
Graphics Equipment (one time only)		15,000[f]
Printing (will change if internal unit is established)	1,000	3,000
TOTAL	$96,500	$264,000
Printing Operations[g]		
Equipment	$15,000–$60,000	
Staff	$12,000	
Supplies (includes service contracts)	$15,000	

[a] Since needs and salaries will vary from institution to institution, the positions, salaries, and items listed above should be considered for reference only and are at starting levels. Budget does not cover technical support (television, audio, basic graphics), audiovisual services, or furniture that already exist on most campuses.

[b] Director will serve part-time in development function.

[c] Includes academic year and summer stipends; tuition not included.

[d] Includes office copier, microcomputer for word processing capabilities for each secretary and professional staff member, and printer; one-time-only expenditure.

[e] Includes additional microcomputer systems for word processing networking capabilities and a laser printer for desk-top publishing (8 stations).

[f] Includes computer system for graphic support.

[g] All expenses may be affected by income.

port components are not included, graphic artist positions are added at Level II since experience has shown that the need for these services grows rapidly as the number of projects increases. The establishment of a computer-based desk-top publishing capability is strongly recommended by Level II. We have found a network system connected to a laser printer particularly efficient. CID has selected a Macintosh AppleTalk network to fulfill the diverse needs it has for publishing, graphics, and data handling.

Additional Space Requirements for Independent Learning

Although some courses, particularly laboratories using such approaches as the Keller Plan or audiotutorial format, are taught entirely on a self-instructional mode, in many more instances independent study is appropriate for only a small portion of the total course. These portions may cover a broad range: from programmed remedial units in mathematics and English to tape/slide sequences in drama and nutrition to audio segments in music, history, foreign languages, computer simulation in sociology and political science, and interactive video units in nursing and engineering.

Therefore, a supervised independent learning facility should be established for use by all academic areas. Such a facility, located within the library or as a separate entity, has several additional advantages.

- It can be used to field test and evaluate new units under controlled conditions.
- Staff of the laboratory can also administer posttests when the units are used for remediation.
- It allows many departments to share cost effectively the same space and equipment.

The need for supervision with the field testing of new materials makes it essential that a facility of this type be self-contained. For this reason, the Syracuse laboratory is not located within the library. Once the units are operational, however, many of the less complex ones are moved into the media areas of the university library, where they are available during open hours.

Since technology is constantly changing, as are the instructional demands of the faculty, the stations should be made as flexible as possible, allowing the capabilities of the station to change as needed. Generally, carrels fall into three types: audiovisual, video, and computer. We have found that carrels with built-in audio cassette decks to which rear projection 35-mm slide or 16-mm projection can be added meet most general audiovisual needs. A larger area, in which up to three or four students can view video tapes using earphones, meets the video needs, while every two computer stations share a printer. As previously noted, the audiovisual stations should, with the exception of the audio tape decks, be equipped only with the specific equipment that is needed at that time. This approach significantly reduces the cost of establishing the laboratory. With the heavy demand on many campuses for computer stations, we suggest using the laboratory only for sequences undergoing field testing and requiring close supervision and for the more complex application in which the computer is being used with other equipment, video tape or video discs, and so on. While the number of stations will, of course, vary from institution to institution, a forty- to fifty-station laboratory that can be supervised easily will provide a great deal of flexibility and a strong potential for instructional applications.

Additional Impact on Programs

These examples have focused on helping existing programs and offices; in two instances the efforts of the center have resulted in establishing new programs.

Project Advance. Project Advance grew out of the recognition by high school administrators of two problematic situations: (1) duplication of curriculum between the last two years of high school and the first two years of college, and (2) "senioritis" or senior-year boredom among capable high school students who have completed most of their graduation requirements by the end of their junior year. In 1972, concerns like these led a group of high school administrators in the Syracuse area to contact the university for assistance. The problem was turned over to the director of the center to explore ways in which the university might cooperate with the schools in developing a solution.

After considering most of the alternatives that have usually been employed in school-college programs, that is, (1) "split-day" programs, in which students divide their time between the high school and college campuses, (2) college courses taught within the school by college faculty, (3) early graduation, and (4) the Advanced Placement Examination Program, the director decided to explore ways in which carefully designed and controlled university courses could be taught for credit within the high school by high school teachers as part of the school's regular academic program. The care with which key freshman courses (English, calculus, psychology, sociology, and so on) had been designed in the center made this approach possible.

As the idea of Project Advance developed, the rationale for the program was extended and refined. It included the general rationale described earlier: reduce curriculum duplication and challenge high school seniors. In practice, however, the project has come to serve perhaps an even more important purpose. It is clearly a proving ground for college-bound seniors, a unique opportunity for them to gauge their ability to do college work and to sharpen their academic and management skills in preparation for college itself. In addition, it has provided college professors and seasoned high school faculty with a continual forum for instructional development in several important content areas.

Recognized nationally as a prototype for college/high school cooperation, Project Advance has proved to be effective and efficient, is totally self-supporting with a budget of over $700,000, and has an annual enrollment of over 4,000 students. Courses are offered in over eighty high schools in New York, Maine, Massachusetts, New Jersey, and Michigan. It now includes freshman-level courses in English, calculus, sociology, psychology, religion, chemistry, biology, political science, economics, and computer engineering, with new courses being added as needs are identified.

The Academic Support Center. Almost from its first day of operation, staff at the center became keenly aware that some students enter the institution without the basic skills necessary for success. Working with faculty in the basic English and mathematics courses and with staff from student affairs and the Higher Education Opportunity Program, a series of instructional units were designed and field tested to help eliminate these deficiencies.

During this period, a campus-wide advisory committee was established by the chancellor's office to explore, on an institution-wide basis, how these problems might be further addressed. It was their recommendation that an Academic Support Center be established and that the office be located within the Center for Instructional Development. A modest budget was provided, and work began in the mid 1970s to establish the unit and develop the programs that were required. Extensive work was done in the teaching of writing, basic mathematics, and study skills and in the implementation of workshops, tutoring programs, seminars, and a summer program (Running Start) for the poorly prepared entering college student. Several years ago, to improve the unit's efficiency, the Academic Support Center, with its budget and support staff, was moved to the counseling area of student affairs.

Summary

There is little question that a support agency like CID can play a major supporting role in helping a college or university reach the goals implicit in the various national studies that have called for changes in higher education. The cost is relatively low. What are needed, however, are effective leadership, a talented and dedicated staff, and, equally important, administrative support. In the chapter that follows we will focus on what can be done to help ensure success and survival.

12

Ensuring the Success
of Instructional
Improvement Programs

This chapter presents a review of the specific steps that can be taken to improve the life expectancy of an instructional development agency and the quality and significance of its impact.

Overview

As we look around the country, we find that while some support units have flourished, others, after only a few years of existence, have disappeared from their institution's organization chart, never to be seen again. The factors that differentiate those that have proved successful from those that have not are many: administrative location and level of support, the quality of staff, the political climate in which the support unit was established, how realistic the goals were, how much pure luck was around when it was needed—the list could go on for pages. Luck may play a role, but success is not determined by chance. Some actions reduce the risks of failure, other actions or lack of action may, over time, ensure that problems will be created and impact of the support unit diminished. The question is a basic one: "What action or combination of actions reduces the chances of failure and improves the prognosis for success?" In establishing and directing an instructional development agency, what can be done to increase impact, reduce or eliminate potential problems, and, in the long run, develop accountability?

The best way to answer the question is to learn from experience. As simple as this may sound, learning from experience is not easy. In many instances there is a significant difference between what one reads about a project and what really happened. Major problems are rarely mentioned, and significant decisions are seldom highlighted. In addition, problems related to politics and personalities, while common, will, for obvious reasons, be unreported. Understandably, people do not like to admit that they failed. And yet, some of the best lessons we can learn are from failures, not successes.

In 1984, Steven Sachs, after reviewing the literature on instructional development, identified thirty-eight characteristics of a model agency. Many of these have been discussed in this book: quality planning with a focus on improving instruction rather than encouraging the adoption of any one solution, a formal organization with a quality staff and some discretionary funds, the existence of a procedure for establishing priorities and for involving faculty and administration, and the need to use evaluation.

This chapter is based on scars — scars from mistakes that, made once, should not be repeated. It is designed to be as specific and as helpful as we can write it, with the hope that, having read it, anyone involved in such an agency will make fewer mistakes and develop only superficial scars.

Out on the Proverbial Limb

When resources were plentiful, we were spared the awkward need to evaluate older programs in the light of new ones, of deciding whether those programs no longer central to a university's mission or duplicated nearby should go in order to fund adequately programs of higher priority [Newman, 1982, p. 13].

Anyone familiar with the American system of higher education does not require additional data to be convinced that the next decade will not be an easy one for most colleges and universities. While the anticipated decrease in the pool of college students has not materialized, changes in the student grant and loan programs, reductions in endowment income, diminishing federal and state support, demands for accountability, and the drive toward reducing taxes at both the federal and state levels have all combined to bring a sense of uneasiness to campuses that have long prided themselves on being islands isolated from the world of layoffs, budget reductions, and other fiscal problems.

While few, if any, institutions will close in the next decade, almost every college and university (private and public, large and small, two-year, four-year, and graduate) will probably experience major budgetary problems as increased resources are required to support high technology programs and institution-wide computerization. The increased cost of libraries, health care for employees, insurance, physical plant maintenance, and legal fees will also claim a large share of the available dollars. On every campus, administrators will face the problem of meeting new and increased needs with a basic stable pool of dollars.

As newer units in the institution, instructional development agencies are among the most vulnerable to cuts or elimination. Rarely perceived as an integral part of the traditional university, without a long history and without the obvious mission of the computer center, the audiovisual center, library, admissions, and development offices, instructional development and faculty development offices can expect to be among the first areas for possible reduction or elimination. A Gustafson and Bratton study (1983) of sixty-one instructional improvement centers reported significant budget reduction in well over half between 1975 and 1982. The importance of a unit designed to facilitate the improvement of instruction and the vulnerability of such an agency were highlighted in the summary of the report by the evaluation team of the Commission of Higher Education of the Middle States Association of Colleges and Schools in their November 1977 report on Syracuse University.

> Syracuse has a success story on its hands, namely, the Center for Instructional Development. So-called institutionalized programs aimed at fostering change, innovations, creativity, etc., seldom have much impact on institutions of higher education long accustomed to resisting, subverting, or waiting out the foreign bodies. By contrast CID is recognized as a "change agent" whose contributions are well distributed throughout the instructional programs, mostly undergraduate, of the university. . . . CID has been a creative, helpful influence in many areas of instruction. A good staff with imagination and a necessary trace of common sense has been able to help faculty change and improve their ways of teaching. They have also influenced curricular offerings and have shown some ways to cope with the knotty problems of remedial/developmental instruction. . . . It is the opinion of the evaluation team that the health of units devoted to change is often jeopardized when the requirements for change are greatest. Too often the first to go as "luxuries" when the pressures mount are the vehicles which show some promise of helping others cope with new conditions. A comprehensive institutional planning approach should have a place for some elements preoccupied with pursuing new ways [Commission of Higher Education of the Middle States Association of Colleges and Schools, 1977, p. 10].

Survival Cannot Be Left to Chance

There is little question that when instructional development agencies are effective, they can play a significant role in helping an institution meet the challenge of the next decade.

However, for agencies to maintain their support, two things must occur:

1. The unit must be effective. It must have a positive and significant impact on the instruction.
2. The value of the agency must be understood by the decision makers.

What follows are specific suggestions for action designed to promote the health, effectiveness, and longevity of instructional development centers.

Steps to Survival

Identify the Priorities of the Institution. What is important? Which programs require and merit help? What new areas are to be developed, and where are the programs that require major revision? What institutional commitments to change or improvement have been and are being made; that is, what are the priorities for the next few years? This information can be obtained from

- Publications/reports
- Formal meetings
- Informal conversations
- Public hearings

As you might anticipate, the information you collect may at times be vague and even contradictory. While it is not always an easy task to identify priorities, the first step must be to develop a draft of such a statement.

Once developed, discuss the list with key decision makers, the people whose perception will affect the future of the agency and those to whom the agency reports. Expect to revise and revise again. From this list, identify those statements where substantial agreement exists. It is these sets of institutional goals that will determine the priorities of the agency. If there are instances in which you seriously question the logic of what you have found, or you feel that major elements have been omitted, or that there appears to be substantial development among those who have provided you with information, it is the ideal time to bring these concerns to the attention of key administrators.

Identify the Key Decision Makers. How often academic units fail to identify those individuals who will be most important in deciding whether or not their particular operation should be supported, reduced, or eliminated! This group includes

- Administrator(s) to whom the unit directly reports
- Other administrators and administrative aides
- Deans and department chairpersons with whom the unit works (including those who have the responsibility for the courses and programs that are being supported)
- Faculty being served
- Faculty and staff on key committees (advisory, academic affairs, curriculum, and so on)
- Unofficial opinion leaders and other respected faculty

Identify the Criteria the Decision Makers Will Use to Judge the Value and Success of the Agency. We often know surprisingly little about the factors that others use in determining our worth. Several years ago the Center at Syracuse developed and field tested an instrument (see Resource E) to help the staff of various academic support units to identify the criteria that various individuals use to judge their work. (A review of this instrument can be found in the Winter 1979 issue of *Planning for Higher Education.* See Cohn, 1979.)

It soon became apparent with the field testing of this instrument that on many campuses not only do staff of the agencies make incorrect assumptions but in some instances they emphasize activities that are not particularly significant to the institution. Others collect and provide the wrong kind of information in their reports. It was found, for example, that while the directors of faculty development offices set one kind of goals for their units (large number of faculty served, improved faculty attitudes, publications by staff, and so on), the administrators to whom they report are interested in impact on attrition and recruitment—factors not mentioned by a single director. At one institution an academic improvement agency was voted out of existence by the faculty who perceived that the unit placed more emphasis on developing a national reputation than on providing them service.

    In 1975, an evaluation of the Syracuse Center was made by the Senate Academic Planning Committee. The questions that were raised by this faculty committee are representative of the questions that can be anticipated in any faculty review of an instructional development agency.

1. Briefly, what is the project on which you worked collaboratively with CID, and how successful do you believe it was?
2. What skills did CID bring to the collaboration?
3. How important was the money CID provided in support of your project?
4. Could you have carried out your project without CID? Explain.
5. Would you have carried out your project without CID? Explain.
6. Does your department see CID as itself an advocate of specific methods for carrying out instruction, or as a neutral catalyst for the discovery and exploration of ideas by the faculty?
7. Have there been sequels to, or spin-offs from, your CID-related project in your department, influenced by the project but carried out without CID help? If so, what are they, and do you think they have been positive developments?
8. What have been the financial and efficiency outcomes of your CID collaboration: same impact for less money? more impact for same money? more impact for more money? less impact for more money?
9. Are you planning to turn again to CID for help? Would you recommend CID to other departments? Unconditionally? Conditionally?

10. How do you think other departments and other faculty
     members see CID? Why?

While some administrators tend to resist being specific in
listing the criteria they use, the fact that one asks the questions
so that he or she can better serve the institution usually helps to
get over this hurdle. The key questions are

- What criteria are being used to judge the agency's worth?
- Which of these criteria are deemed most important?

*Develop Goals That Meet These Criteria, and Make Sure
That They Are Clearly Defined and Can Be Measured.* If goals of
various decision makers differ and, in addition, are not compatible with those of the center's staff, try to reach some agreement.
This often requires discussions and some significant change of
attitudes on both sides. However, without basic agreement, the
agency is totally vulnerable to the charge that its work is not
particularly important to the institution.

- Can agreement be reached among the key decision makers
  as to which criteria are most important?
- What type of data/support information do the decision
  makers want; that is, what are they looking for?

When some disagreement as to priorities still remains, it
is the responsibility of the administrator of the unit to determine, usually with the help of others, which specific goals are
selected for emphasis and maximum rapport. It is also extremely important, whatever the goals, that one can determine
when they are reached. Vague, unmeasurable goals can make
demonstrating the success of any agency difficult.

Select Projects with Care. Avoid spending a great deal of
time doing things that may be enjoyable and personally rewarding but that are of low priority to the institution. If at all possible,
the projects selected should

- Relate directly to the priorities that have been established
- Meet the criteria established by the decision makers
- Be cost effective
- Have a good chance of success

Project selection is no easy task. It requires care not only in selecting what will be undertaken but also in the selection of the faculty with whom the staff will work. The projects that are supported must be both successful and efficiently conducted, and they must meet the priorities established for the unit. It is extremely important that goals of the unit are realistic and that *every* promise made is kept.

The specific factors that should be considered in the selection of a project for development were discussed earlier in Chapter Three. As noted in the discussion of the selection process there are times when, as a result of administrative pressure, high-risk projects must be undertaken. In these instances, the anticipated problems and risks should be identified and brought to the attention of the administrator requesting action. Perhaps most important of all factors is the selection of the specific faculty who will be involved, for without dedicated and competent faculty a project cannot succeed.

Those Who Need to Know Must Be Kept Informed. All of the individuals identified as decision makers must be kept informed of what is happening and what the results of projects are. For some, this has to be on a weekly basis; for others, monthly or perhaps just once or twice a year. All too often, project staff keep administrators and chairpersons of key committees in the dark only to find out, when their support is solicited, that they do not appreciate surprises or may have valid objections or concerns about the project—concerns that could easily have been taken care of if they had been contacted earlier and involved. Many fine ideas have been shot down because of a breakdown in communications.

Many channels of communication are available. These include

- Formal reports (focusing on what the reader is interested in knowing)
- Informal reports—delivered in person, perhaps with brief summary handouts
- Informal conversations
- Selected distribution of the materials that were produced
- Selected distribution of journals and other materials that contain appropriate and significant information

In addition, staff should not overlook the power of positive informal comments made to colleagues by faculty and administrators who have worked with the unit and received its services.

Be Cost Effective and of Modest Size. It is crucial that the agency be perceived as being worth the money that is invested in it. The greater the impact for the fewer dollars being invested, the greater the chance of long-range stability. The development agency should never become so large that internal communications begin to suffer and the agency's budget becomes an automatic target for committees and administrators searching for dollars or budget cuts. Although the point at which a budget becomes vulnerable varies from institution to institution, an investment of from $250,000 to $300,000 for instructional development and evaluation purposes in a large institution seems to be a realistic bench mark. This figure is *above* that allotted to the audiovisual and production support activities traditionally available on most campuses.

Have Realistic Goals. When a unit is established, its staff should not make commitments they will be unable to keep. Promise less and deliver more rather than develop unrealistic expectations. Those responsible for running a new unit should make sure they have enough time to do what is expected of them. Remember that projects often become far more complex than at first anticipated and to promise early implementation and impact is extremely risky. Once an agency loses credibility, it is almost impossible to gain it back.

Keep a Low Profile. Although it is always nice to have people know the agency exists, extensive advertising too soon

may create major problems for the unit and unrealistic expectations—more demands than the unit can possibly meet. If the
staff is already overcommitted, the unit cannot afford to adver-
tise its services. It may be necessary, due to staff limitations, to
have some projects moving slower than others, but the agency
must avoid building up a backlog of requests that are impossible
to meet.

Have a Procedure and Follow It. There are almost as many
models for instructional development as there are instructional
developers. We prefer the sequence detailed in this book, but
there are other approaches. What is important is that the staff
select one that they find appropriate and use it. Agreeing on an
approach ensures that all the critical questions will be addressed and also that everyone involved knows where they are in
the process, where they are going, and what their roles are.

Begin at the Beginning. Do not skip steps. Unless assumptions about the students, the content, and the structure are
tested, the staff has no way of knowing if what they are doing or
improving should be done in the first place. In addition, the
more "givens" a team starts with, the less chance they have of
being successful.

Emphasize Major Projects. If the agency desires to have
impact on the students and the academic program, the focus
must be on courses and curricula. Working on individual
lessons or parts of courses, in laboratories, or on teaching styles,
or focusing on media design and production will keep the staff
busy, but over time these efforts have little impact on the structure and scope of the programs and on what students learn.

Be Sensitive to Human Problems. A center cannot be successful unless it has a staff sensitive to the needs, interests, and
concerns of a number of groups.

- *The decision makers:* Make sure they are involved, know what is
  going on, and have ownership.
- *The faculty:* It is never easy to have someone constantly checking our assumptions, identifying our faults, and making
  sure we keep up with the required work. Course and curriculum design is hard work. An effective development center

does everything it can to provide support, eliminate unnecessary frustration, and reduce the static an innovative faculty member may receive from other faculty.

- *The students:* Be sensitive to the problem of the students in a course or program that is being offered for the first time or is undergoing revision. Everything may not be working well, the work load may be excessive, and every other day someone collects evaluation data. Keep the students informed, let them know their assistance and patience are important, and be prepared to adjust and modify the course on the basis of their responses.

Have a Realistic Reward System. Explore all alternatives for building the design activity into the formal reward system (tenure, promotion, salary increments) for faculty. Assist the faculty member in publishing reports and studies relating to the project and in getting on the program as a speaker at regional and state meetings. Develop a royalty procedure, and help the faculty in any way possible to gain recognition for what they have done. Make sure that the key decision makers are aware of these accomplishments.

Do Not Reinvent the Wheel. Whenever possible, use some of the course and curriculum designs and evaluation instruments we have presented in this book for reference. Using existing media and external publications is a lot cheaper and certainly faster. Keep abreast of what is new, what is being tried, and, if it is helpful in the project, use it. Do not waste resources by doing what has already been done.

Pay Attention to Support Systems and Logistics. The registrar's office, perhaps more than any other, can encourage or discourage academic innovation by being supportive or obstructive to change. The library also can play a large role. Since faculty have a tendency not to worry about logistics — scheduling, room assignments, book orders, multiple sets of materials, and number of computer terminals, an effective center makes sure that communications are established and all student needs are met. Do not leave things to chance. If structured time or credit changes are being discussed, involve the registrar from the beginning.

Keep Media in Perspective. Do not select the solution before identifying the problem and exploring the alternatives. When technology is used, make sure it is the best solution and that what is being used is well done. Careful selection is essential. When properly used, technology can be a major asset in improving instructional quality and effectiveness. All too often we find faculty and staff starting with the answers and then attempting to modify the project accordingly—a process that usually leads to poor results and failure.

Build in Evaluation. An effective evaluation program can significantly improve the quality of the program under development. Data provide a base for good decision making throughout a project. If possible, collect data on the students and the program before work begins so that base information for comparative studies is available. Determine what information is needed, and develop an evaluation system that provides this information. Remember, evaluation data not only improve the quality of individual projects but also can be extremely helpful in justifying the existence of the agency staff. If requested by the faculty member, the data can be provided to tenure and promotion committees as evidence of his or her teaching effectiveness and efforts in this area.

Expect the Unexpected. There are power failures, people get sick, boxes get lost, students may not bother to listen to what they are told or read materials they are given. A snowstorm can play havoc with a schedule in place for months, and a computer system always manages to be down on the most crucial day of the year. We have had guest speakers miss their planes and the faculty member scheduled to handle the major course orientation end up having a baby on that day—two months early. At times like these, one can only do his or her best, be creative, and retain a sense of humor—there are times when that is all that is left.

Summary

Obviously, a list like this is never complete. Many of the suggestions, once one thinks about them, are obvious. The problem is that many of the problems we find we have created ourselves—by rushing, by not worrying about details, by not listening, or by not being as sensitive to the feelings of others as we should be.

Ultimately the success of an instructional development agency is measured by the success of others—the students and the faculty.

In facing the challenges of the next decade, *agency survival cannot be left to chance.* We must recognize that there will be a direct relationship between the homework that is done, the quality of the unit, the impact it has, and its potential for survival. An agency that does not effectively meet the needs of those it serves will not and should not survive.

Resources

A. Sample Agreement for Copyright
    of Instructional Materials
    and Student Manuals

B. Sample Alumni Survey for Evaluating
    Program Effectiveness and Needs

C. Statement of Cross-Disciplinary
    Educational Outcomes: Qualities
    of the Liberally Educated Person

D. Questions to Consider
    in Evaluating a College Course

E. Sample Questionnaire
    for Use in Planning Evaluations
    of Programs and Agencies

Resource A.
Sample Agreement for Copyright
of Instructional Materials
and Student Manuals

This is an Agreement made on_____between

_____residing at_____

_____ ("Author") and SYRACUSE UNIVERSITY, a not-for-

profit educational institution located in Syracuse, New York ("University")

1.   Recitals.

(a) Author is the author of certain written materials which were developed with the

support of the University's Center for Instructional Development ("Center").

(b) Author desires to have the materials published and the University is willing to

publish the materials, all as set forth in this Agreement.

2.   Grant of Rights.

(a) The Author hereby grants and assigns to the University the right to publish and

sell worldwide the following material(s):

(i)_____

(ii)_____

(iii)_____

(iv)_____

(referred to as "Work" or "Works")

(b)   The University shall publish the Work at its own expense in such style and

manner as it deems appropriate. the University shall have the sole right and authority to determine the number of issues to be published and the terms and manner of the sale of the Work.

(c)   The University is under no obligation to keep the Work in print. In the event all of the printed copies of the Work are sold, the University shall have the right to determine, at its own discretion, whether to print additional copies.

(d)   The parties agree that they will jointly promote the sale of the Work in such manner as they shall determine. The University shall not be under any obligation to promote the sale of the Work except as otherwise agreed by the parties.

3.   Royalties.

(a)   The University shall pay to the Author a royalty of 15% of the University's selling price, less any discounts, returns and sales tax, of every copy of the Work sold by the University, unless rights to royalties are waived by the Author in writing. If more than one author has contributed to the Work, the 15% royalty shall be split among the contributing authors with the Author receiving the following portion:

<u>Item</u>	<u>Percent</u>
(i)	_____
(ii)	_____
(iii)	_____
(iv)	_____

(b)   Royalties shall be paid within 60 days after each June 30 and December 31 for the six month period then ended. Royalty payments shall be accompanied by a written statement identifying the number of copies of the Work sold during the period and the total receipts upon which the computation of royalties is based.

(c)   The University is authorized to withhold from royalty payments taxes and other amounts required by law to be withheld.

4.   <u>Manuscript</u>.

The Author authorizes the University to edit and make changes in the manuscript of the Work, provided that all changes in the manuscript are subject to the approval of the Author or, if more than one Author, the approval of the senior Author.

5.   <u>Copies</u>.

The University shall provide the Author free of charge two copies of the published work, with additional copies to be made available to the Author at the University's cost.

One complimentary set of media materials shall also be provided to the Author or, if more than one author, to the senior author.

6.   Commercial Publication.

Notwithstanding the rights granted to the University by this Agreement, either the Author or the University may contract with a commercial publishing house to publish and sell the Work, provided that no such agreement may be entered into without the prior written approval of the other party. In the event an agreement is entered into with a commercial publisher, the royalties payable under that agreement will be divided among the parties as follows, unless otherwise agreed by the parties:

(a)   If the commercial publisher requires revisions which, in the sole judgment of the University, will require a minimum of rewriting by the Author (or authors), the author (or authors), the Author (or authors) will be entitles to 60% of the royalties paid by the commercial publisher and the University will be entitled to the remaining 40%.

(b)   If the commercial publisher requires revisions which, in the sole judgment of the University, will require major rewriting by the Author (or authors), the Author (or authors) will be entitled to 75% of the royalties paid by the commercial publisher, and the University will be entitled to the remaining 25%.

7.   Representations and Warranties.

(a)   The Author represents and warrants to the University as follows:

(i)   With the exception of those other authors who contributed to the Work and who have signed a similar agreement with the University, Author is the sole owner of the Work (other than material prepared by the Center and its staff) and of the rights granted by this Agreement;

(ii)   The Author has not granted proprietary rights in the Work to any other party;

(iii)   The Work is an original creation of the Author and does not contain material copyrighted by others, or, if such copyrighted material is included in the Work, the author has obtained permission to reprint the material in the Work;

(iv)   The Work does not contain any libelous or unlawful matter and does not infringe upon the rights of others.

(b)   The Author will defend with competent counsel, indemnify and hold the University harmless from and against all claims, proceedings, losses, damages, costs, attorneys' fees and expenses arising out of or resulting from the Author's breach of any of the foregoing representations and warranties.

(c)   The University shall be entitled to deduct and offset from royalties to be paid to the Author any damages, costs and expenses, including legal fees, incurred by the University by reason of the Author's breach of any of the foregoing representations and warranties. This remedy shall be in addition to any other remedy provided by law or by this Agreement.

8.   Copyright.

(a)   The parties agree that the University shall own the copyright in the Work and that the Work shall bear a copyright notice in the name of the University upon first publication. The University reserves the right to register the copyright in the U.S. Copyright Office but is under no obligation to do so.

(b)   The University shall have the right at its own expense to enforce any and all copyrights on the Work, to prosecute any infringement of the copyrights, and to retain the proceeds of any such infringement action.

9.   Terms and Termination

(a)   This Agreement shall continue in force and effect for the term of the original U.S. copyright of the Work.

(b)   Notwithstanding the foregoing, the parties may terminate this Agreement as follows:

(i)   the Author may terminate this Agreement at any time after five years;

(ii)   The University may terminate this Agreement at any time it determines there is not sufficient market for the Work to justify continued publication of the Work; provided, however, that any termination of this Agreement will not affect the rights of the parties to receive royalties from any commercial publishing house publishing the Work pursuant to paragraph 6.

(c)   In the event of termination, the rights granted to the University shall revert to the Author except as otherwise provided in this Agreement. The Author shall have the right to buy from the University all copies on hand at the University's cost and the University shall have the right to sell or otherwise dispose of all remaining copies of the Work upon such terms as it deems advisable.

10.   Instructional Use.

The University and its employees shall have the right to use the Work for instructional purposes without payment of any royalty under Paragraph 3, and all sales of the Work to the University, its faculty, staff, and students shall bear no royalty.

11.   Governing Law.

This Agreement shall be governed and construed in accordance with the laws of the State of New York.

12.   Binding Effect.

This Agreement shall be binding upon and shall inure to the benefit of the parties and their successors and assigns.

Social Security #   Author

_____

by:

Syracuse University

SYRACUSE UNIVERSITY

COLLEGE FOR HUMAN DEVELOPMENT

112 SLOCUM HALL | SYRACUSE, NEW YORK 13210

(315) 423-2033

March 1985

Dear Graduate:

We are seeking your help as we begin a comprehensive study to determine the relevancy of our programs in the College for Human Development at Syracuse University. Your views as a graduate of this college are very valuable to us as we seek input from the profession.

There has been increasing discussion of late regarding the rapid changes in our society, the shift from industry to technology and communication, and the need for strategic planning. These are of common concern to industry, social service organizations, and education alike. We must project at least five years ahead in order to best prepare our students for their future careers. Therefore we are asking you to share your perspectives and visions and become part of our team as we seek to accomplish this goal.

We have attached a survey which is divided into four sections:

1) General professional skills and personal traits of undergraduates relevant at the entry level in your profession.

2) Topics and experiences specific to your specialization which you think should be included in the undergraduate curriculum.

3) An opportunity for you to share your vision of the future to help us anticipate changes in your profession for which we need to prepare students.

4) Background information so that we may share the results of our survey with you and also update our records of alumni.

Please know that all information you provide us will remain strictly confidential. If you have any questions about the survey, don't hesitate to call me at (315)423-2033, or write to me. I have enclosed a stamped envelope for your convenience. Please return the survey by April 15, 1985, a date that should be easy to remember! And, if you complete and return the enclosed lottery ticket with your survey by April 15th, you will be eligible to win one of five exciting prizes such as a Syracuse University ceramic mug, paperweight or letter opener.

In closing, I would like to once again stress how very important your input is to us. You are in a unique position because of your education and professional experience to directly affect the quality of the educational experience provided by our college. Thank you for your help!

Sincerely,

Jane M. Lillestol
Dean

225

ALUMNI SURVEY
COLLEGE FOR HUMAN DEVELOPMENT
SYRACUSE UNIVERSITY

SECTION I

There are some things that students learn that are not part of the formal academic curriculum. These include general professional skills. In addition, there are personal traits that can be important in one's success in a given area. In response to the following items, please indicate (1), if the skill or trait is important for people in your area and, (2), its prevalence among those people who, like our undergraduates, are just entering your area.   (6)

Professional Skills

Skills	Importance for people in your area					Prevalence among those entering your area				
	none	low	medium	high		none	low	medium	high	
professional writing	0	1	2	3	(7)	0	1	2	3	(16)
professional speaking	0	1	2	3		0	1	2	3	
basic mathematics	0	1	2	3		0	1	2	3	
microcomputer use	0	1	2	3		0	1	2	3	
resource management	0	1	2	3		0	1	2	3	
planning	0	1	2	3		0	1	2	3	
decision making	0	1	2	3		0	1	2	3	
leadership	0	1	2	3		0	1	2	3	
interpersonal skills	0	1	2	3	(15)	0	1	2	3	(24)

Personal Traits

Traits	Importance for people in your area					Prevalence among those entering your area				
	none	low	medium	high		none	low	medium	high	
loyalty	0	1	2	3	(25)	0	1	2	3	(34)
common sense	0	1	2	3		0	1	2	3	
ethics	0	1	2	3		0	1	2	3	
persuasiveness	0	1	2	3		0	1	2	3	
creativity	0	1	2	3		0	1	2	3	
enthusiasm	0	1	2	3		0	1	2	3	
willingness to take risks	0	1	2	3		0	1	2	3	
industriousness	0	1	2	3		0	1	2	3	
appearance	0	1	2	3	(33)	0	1	2	3	(42)

A. There are many topics that could be included in the undergraduate curriculum. From your point of view, how valuable are the topics listed under each of the following categories in the education of an undergraduate preparing to enter your field? Please *circle* the number which most accurately reflects the value you place on each topic. *2 (43)*

Categories/Topics	Value (Circle appropriate number)				
	none	low	medium	high	

RETAILING
(Please rate the following if this is your field.)

retailing fundamentals	0	1	2	3	*(44)*
merchandising mathematics	0	1	2	3	
merchandising management	0	1	2	3	
visual merchandising	0	1	2	3	
salesmanship	0	1	2	3	
retailing problems & policy	0	1	2	3	
small business administration	0	1	2	3	
advertising principles	0	1	2	3	
visual arts	0	1	2	3	
retail advertising	0	1	2	3	
financial accounting	0	1	2	3	
computer applications	0	1	2	3	
data processing	0	1	2	3	
introduction to the legal system	0	1	2	3	
marketing and society	0	1	2	3	
consumers and the marketplace	0	1	2	3	
elementary statistics	0	1	2	3	*(60)*

CONSUMER STUDIES
(Please rate these topics if this is your field.)

individual/family resource management	0	1	2	3	*(61)*
personal finance management	0	1	2	3	
consumer behavior	0	1	2	3	
consumer economics	0	1	2	3	
consumer protection	0	1	2	3	
current consumer issues	0	1	2	3	
consumer education	0	1	2	3	
consumer problems of the elderly	0	1	2	3	*(68)*

SECTION II, CONT.

Categories/Topics	Value (Circle appropriate number)				
	none	**low**	**medium**	**high**	
OTHER CONSUMER STUDIES RELATED TOPICS (Please rate these topics if this is your field.)					
organizational behavior	0	1	2	3	*(69)*
advertising principles	0	1	2	3	
introduction to the legal system	0	1	2	3	
marketing and society	0	1	2	3	
state and national legislative process	0	1	2	3	
computer applications	0	1	2	3	*(74)*
HUMAN DEVELOPMENT TOPICS (Please rate if you are in either field.)					
child and family studies	0	1	2	3	*(75)*
human behavior	0	1	2	3	
human nutrition	0	1	2	3	*(77)*
ARTS AND SCIENCES (Please rate if you are in either field.)					
history	0	1	2	3	*(78)*
higher mathematics (e.g., algebra)	0	1	2	3	
psychology	0	1	2	3	*(80)*
English literature	0	1	2	3	*(6)*
expository writing	0	1	2	3	
foreign language	0	1	2	3	
economics	0	1	2	3	
sociology	0	1	2	3	
anthropology	0	1	2	3	
fine arts	0	1	2	3	
philosophy	0	1	2	3	
religion	0	1	2	3	
chemistry	0	1	2	3	
physics	0	1	2	3	
biology	0	1	2	3	*(17)*

SECTION II, CONT.

B. Entry Level Criteria

1. What are the basic requirements and the outstanding or unique factors that you use to assess an entry level *portfolio?*

basic requirements: _____ *(28)*

_____ *(29)*

_____ *(30)*

outstanding/unique factors: _____ *(31)*

_____ *(32)*

_____ *(33)*

2. What are the basic and outstanding or unique *design capabilities* that you look for in assessing an entry level applicant?

basic capabilities: _____ *(34)*

_____ *(35)*

_____ *(36)*

outstanding/unique capabilities: _____ *(37)*

_____ *(38)*

_____ *(39)*

C. Additional Topics

Are there other topics related to any of the above categories that you feel should be covered in our programs? (Please list them below).

_____ *(40)*

_____ *(41)*

_____ *(42)*

_____ *(43)*

_____ *(44)*

_____ *(45)*

SECTION II, CONT.

D. Practical Experiences

The curriculum also consists of practical experiences as part of a field internship or some other practicum. Please answer the following questions about the field based part of the curriculum.

How important is a field experience in an undergraduate's preparation? (circle one)

| not very important | important | very important | *(46)* |
| 1 | 2 | 3 | |

In your opinion what are the most important elements of a practical field experience?

a. _____ *(47)*

b. _____ *(48)*

c. _____ *(49)*

d. _____ *(50)*

e. _____ *(51)*

E. General Comments and Suggestions

Please make any additional comments or suggestions which you think would help us strengthen our programs for the preparation of undergraduates who will enter your field.

(52)

(53)

(54)

(55)

(56)

Your View of the Future

Next year's freshmen will enter your field five years from now. Therefore, we need to be aware of trends that will have an impact on the field when these students graduate. Please respond to each of the following questions so that we can have the benefit of your perspective as we continue to improve our curriculum to make it relevant to the future.

1. In what direction do you see your profession moving during the next five years?

(57)

(58)

(59)

2. What new knowledge, skills and attitudes will be needed by people entering your field?

(60)

(61)

(62)

3. What skills, attitudes or knowledge will become obsolete and, therefore, no longer needed?

(63)

(64)

(65)

4. What do you see as the essential philosophy and/or components of a program preparing undergraduates to enter your field?

(66)

(67)

(68)

5. Please make any additional comments or suggestions which you think will help us understand your perspective.

(69)

(70)

(71)

SECTION IV

Information about You

Please provide the following information so that we may update our records and share the results of the survey with you. Of course, your response to the survey will be kept confidential.

Name _____
         Last   First   Middle   Maiden

Home Address _____Telephone _____
                   Street   City   State   Zip

Current Business
Address _____Telephone _____
            Street   City·   State   Zip

Undergraduate Major _____ (72) Year Graduated_____ (73-74)

Degree Received _____Institution _____

Additional Degrees - Indicate Major, Institution, and Year Received

_____

Information on Present Status

Please check appropriate category:

_____ Student (1)   _____ Full-time homemaker (2)   (75)

_____ Employed (3)   _____ Retired (4)

_____ Other (Please explain): _____ (5)

Please complete below in regard to most recent employer.

Organization _____
                 Name   Address   City   State   Zip

Period worked for this organization _____

Job Title _____ (76-77)

Describe briefly, the nature of the organization's operation and your position.

_____ (78-79)

_____

_____

_____

Thank you for your help! Please return this survey in the enclosed, stamped envelope or send it to:

> Dr. Peter J. Gray
> Associate in Evaluation
> Syracuse University
> Center for Instructional Development
> 115 College Place
> Syracuse, New York 13210

Resource C.
Statement of Cross-Disciplinary Educational Outcomes: Qualities of the Liberally Educated Person

Qualities of the Liberally Educated Person

A Description of Important Competencies

The Task Force on the Student Experience
Faculty of Arts and Sciences-Newark

233

Members

Lion F. Gardiner, Zoology and Physiology, *Chairman*
John Faulstich, Dean of Instruction, NCAS
Richard H. Kimball, Business Administration
Cassie E. Miller, Dean of Students, UC
Vincent Santarelli, Physics
Harold I. Siegel, Psychology
Raymond T. Smith, Director, Educational
   Opportunity Fund Program
Cecile R. Stolbof, Dean of Instruction, UC
Linda Swanger, Student, NCAS
Elena E. Thompson, Student, UC

Former Members

Henry A. Christian, English
Mary C. Segers, Political Science
Olga J. Wagenheim, History

April 1986

Resource C: Statement of Cross-Disciplinary Outcomes 235

TABLE OF CONTENTS

Introduction

Liberal arts colleges have historically taught a broad range of traditional studies in the humanities, social and natural sciences, and mathematics. This curriculum has recognized the central importance for success in life of broad development of the "whole person" as contrasted with acquisition of career-oriented knowledge and skills alone. Thorough personal development can enable us effectively to plan, control, and enjoy our lives, and it can significantly enhance the probability of professional success and satisfaction as well.

The major human dimensions—intellectual, moral, emotional, and social—all require development. Truly liberal learning can help us develop each of these dimensions, illuminate their interconnections, and reveal their relevance for our lives. When such learning occurs in college, it is accomplished by active involvement with members of the faculty and staff, peers, and others; in and out of class; and on and off campus.

Becoming liberally educated can enable us to identify alternative goals for our lives. It can accelerate our progress in achieving clear and mature personal values and enhance our ability to plan our lives and solve personal and professional problems. Perhaps most important, liberal education can catalyze a process of continuous learning and personal development throughout life.

The more closely the qualities of the liberally educated person are identified, the more easily they can be observed and measured. The description below can guide faculty members and administrators in decision making as they plan, implement, and evaluate curricular and cocurricular activities and assess student achievement. This description can guide students in planning their educational experiences and in assessing their personal change and growth.

The Qualities

These qualities, characteristics, abilities, or competencies involve the whole person and are teachable and measurable. These competencies, although they may be developed in one context, are transferable to other settings and situations and are broadly applicable in life. They are stated in language that permits their observation and measurement.

The qualities are grouped together in four clusters of related competencies. The number of competencies classed together in a cluster in no way signifies the relative importance of the cluster; other classifications are possible.

Specifically, the liberally educated person engages in the following activities:

Cluster I.   Higher-order Cognitive Skills[1]

A. Analytic thinking

1. Draws reasonable inferences from observations and logical premises.

2. Independently discerns internal structure, pattern, and organization using frameworks or models from various disciplines and fields of inquiry to comprehend the natural world, social and cultural relations, and artistic products.

3. Recognizes and analyzes problems in a variety of situations, both independently and cooperatively with others; views issues from a multiplicity of perspectives.

4. Analyzes and describes the value structure of a specific area of knowledge, both in theory and practice.

B. Synthetic-creative thinking

1. Identifies problems, perceives associations, and constructs relationships that are novel.

2. Uses one's intellectual skills effectively to construct original ideas and products.

---

[1] These skills involve the ability to move beyond knowledge requiring memory alone, comprehension, and low-level application of concepts and principles. These skills involve the ability to engage in abstract problem-solving behavior in many settings and contexts.

C. Evaluative thinking

1. Identifies assumptions and limitations in problem solving and evaluates the adequacy of one's own and other's approaches to problems.

2. Evaluates one's own and others' ideas, behavior, and cultures using criteria from various disciplines and fields of inquiry.

D. Scientific reasoning

1. Demonstrates an understanding of the scientific method of inquiry, including accurate measurement based on observation and the use of controlled experiment.

2. Identifies the assumptions and limitations of the scientific method of inquiry and distinguishes the extent to which this method is applicable in various situations and contexts in all disciplines and fields of inquiry.

3. Distinguishes first- from second-hand information, facts from opinions, and hypotheses from substantiated conclusions; identifies the need for and role of appropriate evidence in providing support for or in falsifying testable hypotheses or points of view.

4. Evaluates the quality of evidence, distinguishing appropriate and significant evidence from inadequate evidence, and discriminates between pseudoscientific and scientific explanations.

E. Using numerical data

1. Uses numerical data effectively to provide support for positions taken.

2. Responds in a sophisticated manner to arguments and positions depending on numerical support; recognizes the misuse of numerical data and their manipulation to mislead in the presentation of issues.

Cluster II. Active Awareness of One's Natural Environment

A. Structure and function

Perceives and describes the complex relations of the structures and functions within the physical and organic environment and the relative stability of these relations through time.

B. Human-environment interactions

Observes and analyzes the impact of individuals and groups on the environment, including the role played by technology, and how the environment affects individuals and groups.

C. Problem solving

Constructs effective solutions to environmental problems.

Cluster III. Active Awareness of Oneself

A. Self-identity

1. Articulates a clear and integrated sense of one's own personal identity, place in the world, and potential as a person.

2. Recognizes and names one's own emotional states in various contexts, situations, and circumstances.

3. Demonstrates ability to function effectively under conditions of ambiguity, uncertainty, and conflict.

4. Demonstrates ability to empathize with others who are substantially dissimilar from oneself and to communicate effectively this empathy to others.

5. Demonstrates awareness of the structure and function of one's own body and the conditions that will maintain and ensure its well being.

B. Values

1. Identifies one's own chosen values, and employs consciously these values in decision making in one's own life to take and defend reasoned stands on significant social issues.

2. Demonstrates facility in recognizing and evaluating values expressed in discourse such as casual conversation and in philosophical, political, artistic, and humanistic works and implied by scientific and technological developments.

C. Learning

1. Identifies one's own preferred learning styles and one's strengths and weaknesses as a learner.

2. Demonstrates active, diverse, and effective learning behaviors appropriate to various disciplines and fields of inquiry as an individual and in group settings.

3. Learns independently, both to satisfy one's own curiosity and to achieve practical ends; has an active, consistent, and life-long orientation toward learning.

Cluster IV.   Awareness of and Effective Action in One's Social and Cultural Environment

A. Communication

1. Analyzes oneself as a communicator and identifies one's own strengths and weaknesses.

2. Communicates effectively both abstract concepts and feelings and emotions in writing, speaking, reading, and listening, using words or quantified data, and with other media, including the computer.

3. Identifies and effectively uses the tactics of skilled persuasion; recognizes attempts at manipulation such as hucksterism and demagoguery in various settings, contexts, and situations.

B. Interpersonal interaction

1. Identifies and evaluates one's own behaviors and emotional responses experienced when interacting with others, both in one-to-one and group settings and contexts, and can analyze the behavior of others.

2. Employs effective interpersonal and intragroup behavior when interacting with others in a variety of situations, within one's own culture and in intercultural settings, contexts, and situations.

3. Facilitates effective interpersonal and group interactions both within one's own culture and in intercultural settings, contexts, and situations.

C. Leadership

1. Demonstrates independence of thought in decision making and implements these decisions in an effective way.

2. Demonstrates knowledge of leadership skills and can identify one's own strengths and weaknesses as a leader.

3. Uses effective leadership behaviors confidently in relating to others.

4. Identifies values implicit in political views espoused and methods employed.

D. The contemporary world

1. Demonstrates insight into the psychodynamic forces at work in individuals and groups and utilizes these insights to interpret human events and comprehend their causes, effects, and implications.

2. Demonstrates perception and knowledge of contemporary world conditions and events and the capacity to analyze the complex interrelationships of these conditions and events in their historical contexts.

3. Demonstrates understanding of the growing interdependence of nations, especially concerning natural resources and economic development, and analyzes the impact of events in one area or culture on others.

4. Demonstrates understanding of the structural and functional differences among cultures, Western and Eastern, industrialized and less developed.

5. Based on one's own values, takes and defends effectively a reasoned personal position concerning the implications of contemporary events on various social groups and on one's own personal life.

E. Cultural change

1. Describes the process of cultural change and analyzes specific cultural changes.

2. Evaluates the significance of these cultural changes (1) for individuals and groups, both within a culture and as it relates to other cultures, and (2) the effects of individual and group change on culture.

3. Identifies and evaluates one's own changes over time and one's own response to cultural change.

4. Demonstrates intellectual flexibility and the capacity to adapt to change in one's own life and invarious settings, contexts, and situations.

F. Artistic response and expression

1. Expresses personal response to the literary, performance, and visual arts in terms of their formal elements and one's own personal background.

2. Distinguishes among artistic forms in terms of their elements and one's personal response to specific works.

3. Relates works to their philosophical, historical, and cultural contexts.

4. Makes and defends judgments of the artistic quality of specific works.

5. Expresses creatively both abstract concepts and feelings and emotions using various artistic modes.

Using the Qualities to Develop Curriculum

College faculties and their curriculum committees today are increasingly specifying in considerable detail the learning "outcomes" they desire for their students. The use of "behavioral" language wherever possible increases significantly the probability of actually assessing (measuring) learning, no small advantage today, with a sharply increased awareness of the need for assessment and the demand for accountability.

The "qualities" listed above describe major competencies we consider characteristic of all liberally educated men and women. Although most of these characteristics have been considered important by thinkers for millenia, following increasingly common modern academic practice, they are today written down and couched in precise language to guide the planning and assessment of learning, not to mention the thinking of students themselves.

The curriculum (and today the cocurriculum as well) is the vehicle for actualizing or developing competencies in students. The skilled choice and sequencing of disciplinary content by the teacher in a course, together with the design of activities through which students interact with this content, provide for students the means for developing these competencies.

Caveats

This list of competencies can serve as the nucleus for planning a college curriculum. In doing so, however, several caveats should be noted. First, this list, although representative of what faculties desire for their students, is not exhaustive; each faculty will have its own emphases, greater or lesser, its own degree of desired detail. For example, Quality IV, F, 3 (p. 7), "Relates works to their philosophical, historical, anc cultural contexts," must be significantly elaborated to specify *which* works and specifically *how* these works are to be handled. Are the works literary or in the performing or visual arts? Which are most important? Answering these questions are faculty responsibilities and prerogatives.

These "qualities" are *skills* in general areas; we have not addressed the specific contents of the areas. The content and instructional activities employed to develop these skills are again the province of faculties and their curriculum committees.

Second, although competency statements should be couched in behavioral language wherever possible, it may not be possible to do so in every case. In difficult cases (see Bowen 1977, pp. 53-59, for examples), the competency should be stated as clearly as possible in whatever language one can muster. One should avoid trivializing the complex but not assume that complex learning necessarily cannot be stated clearly and in behavioral language. One should attempt to state competencies even if they cannot at this time be measured.

Third, in developing a curriculum, close attention should be given to linguistic precision, clarity, and consistency. The Alverno College materials cited below may serve as useful guides when writing.

Explanation of the Qualities Clusters

Cluster I. Higher-order Cognitive Skills. The higher-order thinking skills are the means by which we apprehend and control ourselves and our natural and social environment and solve life's problems. These skills comprise the mechanism by which we gain insight into our motivations, consciously shape our behavior, and design our lives. Their practiced use can lead to "wisdom."

Qualities of the Liberally Educated Person   9

The competencies in this cluster are prerequisite to those that follow. They, like the others, are developed through practice, by engaging in abstract problem-solving behavior in many settings, contexts, and situations. The skilled thinker can learn to perform the functions described in the other, succeeding three qualities clusters.

Cluster II.   Active Awareness of One's Natural Environment. We are dependent upon our natural environment for life itself. Our mastery of technology and awareness of its limitations and our understanding and responsible stewardship of our environment are necessary to enable competent decision making that can ensure both the future quality of our own lives and the well-being of other species.

Cluster III. Active Awareness of Oneself. The aphorism "know thyself" articulates a truth known to reflective men and women since antiquity. Success as a person—becoming a "fully functioning person"—requires substantive insight into one's own self: one's self-identity, emotional dynamics, and values. The central importance of self-awareness in life manifests itself by its strongly enhancing effects on the development of the competencies in the other clusters.

Cluster IV.   Awareness of and Effective Action in One's Social and Cultural Environment. For the developed personality, contact with other people is a major part of daily experience.   Understanding others and developing skill in interacting with them is fundamental to achieving one's own goals in life, enjoying other people, and contributing to their lives.

This understanding of others and skill in interacting with them develops through face-to-face practice and reflection and through the use of various media and modes of expression.

Acknowledgements

This description has been developed through an extended review of the professional literature on American liberal arts colleges and the goals they have for their students and the competencies they attempt to develop in them.   Of special help were detailed descriptions of the eight "abilities" forming the core of the Alverno College curriculum (see Alverno College Faculty 1979, 1981; Earley et al. 1980; and Loacker et al. 1984) and competencies developed by the

Tennessee Higher Education Commission (Branscomb 1977). In addition, we have drawn on the recently released reports of the National Institute of Education Study Group on the Conditions of Excellence in American Higher Education (Mortimer 1984) and the Association of American Colleges Select Committee of the Project on Redefining the Meaning and Purpose of Baccalaureate Degrees (Curtis 1985).

The following colleagues graciously read various drafts of this description and offered many valuable criticisms, comments, and suggestions: Drs. Michael I. Aissen (Mathematics), Virginia K. Cremin-Rudd (English), Margaret Furcron (Academic Foundations), Patricia A. Gartenberg (English), Jan E. Lewis (History), Marc A. Mappen (Associate Dean, FAS-N), Douglas W. Morrison (Zoology and Physiology), Mary Lou Motto (English) Louis H. Orzack (Sociology), Lillian Robbins (Psychology), Pheroze S. Wadia (Philosophy), and Ann C. Watts (English).

A number of our quality statements are identical to Alverno College ability statements. We thank Sr. Austin Doherty, Vice President for Academic Affairs of Alverno College, for permission to use them here.

Literature Cited

Alverno College Faculty. 1979. Assessment at Alverno College. Alverno Productions, Milwaukee. 60 pp.

_____. 1981. Liberal Learning at Alverno College. Alverno Productions, Milwaukee. 42 pp.

Bowen, H.R. 1977. Investment in Learning: The Individual and Social Value of American Higher Education. Jossey-Bass, San Francisco. 507 pp.

Pages 53-59, "A Catalog of Goals," provides a taxonomy of college goals for student development summarizing 1,500 goal statements in the literature.

Branscomb, H., O. Milton, J. Richardson, and H. Spivey. 1977. The Competent College Student: An Essay on the Objectives and Quality of Higher Education. Tennessee Higher Education Commission, Nashville. 20 pp.

Curtis, M.H., Chairman. 1985. Integrity in the College Curriculum: A Report to the Academic Community. Association of American Colleges, Washington, D.C. 47 pp.

Earley, M., M. Mentkowski, and J. Schafer. 1980. Valuing at Alverno: The Valuing Process in Liberal Education. Alverno Productions, Milwaukee. 97 pp.

Loacker, G., L. Cromwell, J. Fey, and D. Rutherford. 1984. Analysis and Communication at Alverno: An Approach to Critical Thinking. Alverno Productions, Milwaukee. 189 pp.

Mortimer, K.P., Chairman. 1984. Involvement in Learning: Realizing the Potential of American Higher Education. Final Report of the National Institute of Education Study Group on the Conditions of Excellence in American Higher Education. National Institute of Education, United States Department of Education, Washington, D.C. 99 pp.

Resource D.
Questions to Consider
in Evaluating a College Course

Richard R. Sudweeks and Robert M. Diamond

No two evaluation designs will be the same. In each instance the evaluation must be structured to serve the information needs of those involved in the decision-making process. There is, however, a general list of questions that tend to recur in the evaluation of courses and other programs of instruction. The following list has been designed assist faculty and administrators who are or will be charged with the task of evaluating a course. While no list could ever be considered complete, these items have been developed from efforts on several campuses that have dealt with the design and implementation of new courses and programs as well as the evaluation of existing courses and curricula. The list is intended to be a functional guide in the design stage of an evaluation. It should serve as a checklist making sure that all relevant questions have been considered.

In using this list, it must be remembered that all the questions may not be appropriate in a single project because of limitations in time, staff, and money. It is up to those involved to select the specific questions that should be addressed and to place priorities among them. It is our hope that this list will lead to more responsible decisions regarding which issues will be addressed in the evaluation. Questions which are not included in the evaluation should be omitted intentionally rather than by accident. The evaluation methodology that is elected should match the questions that are being asked.

Following the list you will find an example of the questions selected for use in evaluating two on-going experimental courses (see page 203).

CONSIDER EACH OF THE FOLLOWING QUESTIONS
AND CHECK THOSE THAT ARE APPROPRIATE FOR
THE SPECIFIC COURSE YOU ARE EVALUATING

I.   COURSE RATIONALE

☐   A. What population of students is the course intended to serve?

☐   B. What student needs is the course intended to service?

☐   C. What institutional, community or societal needs is the course intended to serve?

☐   D. What other defensible reasons exist for offering this course?

☐   E. What other courses serve these same needs?

☐   F. To what extent does this course overlap with or duplicate these other courses?

☐   G. On what grounds is the continued existence of this course justified and warranted?

II.   DEVELOPMENT AND CURRENT STATUS OF THE COURSE

☐   A. When and under what circumstances was the course developed?

☐   B. How frequently and how regularly has the course been offered?

☐   C. To what extent has the enrollment increased, decreased or stabilized from year to year?

☐   D. What problems have been associated with the course and how have they been
       resolved?

☐   E. To what extent is the course intended to be replicable from instructor to instructor or
       from term to term?

☐   F. To what degree do the plans or design for the course exist in a written or documented
       form? In what documents (course approval forms, course outlines or syllabi, memos,
       etc.) do these plans exist?

☐   G. How does the current version of the course differ from earlier versions? Why?

III. CREDIT AND CURRICULAR IMPLICATIONS

☐   A. What credit is awarded for successful completion of the course? On what basis is this
       credit allocation justifiable?

☐   B. In what ways can credit for this course be applied towards fulfillment of graduate and
       degree requirements?

☐ C. At what level (lower division, upper division or graduate) is the course classified? Why? On what basis is this classification justified?

☐ D. How does the course fit into the overall curriculum of the sponsoring department and college?

☐ E. In which departments is the course cross-listed? Why? How does it fit into the curriculum of these departments or colleges?

☐ F. What prerequisite skills or experiences are needed in order to succeed in this course?

☐ G. What problems are experienced by students who do not have these prerequisites?

IV.   COURSE OBJECTIVES

☐ A. What are the formal, stated objectives of the course?

☐ B. How feasible and realistic are these objectives in terms of the abilities of the target population and the available time and resources?

☐ C. How are the stated objectives related to the adult life-role competencies students will need in everyday life outside of school?

☐ D. How are the objectives related to the competencies students will need in their subsequent academic careers?

☐ E. If the course is designed to prepare students for a specific professional or vocational field, how are the objectives related to the competencies they are likely to need in their future careers?

☐ F. What values are affirmed by the choice of these objectives as goals for this course?

☐ G. What other purposes, intents, or goals do the faculty, administrators, and other interested audiences have for the course?

☐ H. What goals and expectations do students have for the course?

☐ I. To what extent are these additional goals and expectations compatible with the stated course objectives?

V. THE CONTENT OF THE COURSE

☐ A. What (1) information, (2) processes, and (3) attitudes and values constitute the subject-matter or content of the course?

☐ B. How are the various content elements related to the course's objectives?

    ☐ 1. Which objectives receive the most coverage or emphasis? Why?

    ☐ 2. Which objectives receive only minor coverage? Why?

☐ C. How is the content sequenced or arranged? Why is this sequence appropriate/inappropriate?

☐ D. What means are used to integrate and unify the various content elements into a coherent pattern or structure? To what extent does fragmentation or lack of coherence appear to be a problem?

☐ E. What values and assumptions are implicit in the decisions which have been made regarding content selection and emphasis?

VI.   INSTRUCTIONAL STRATEGIES

☐ A. What kinds of learning activities are utilized?

    ☐ 1. What activities are the students expected to engage in during class sessions?

    ☐ 2. What assignments or projects are students expected to complete outside of class?

    ☐ 3. In what ways are these activities appropriate or inappropriate in light of the course objectives?

    ☐ 4. How could these activities be made more effective?

☐ B. What instructional materials are utilized?

    ☐ 1. How and for what purpose are the materials used?

    ☐ 2. How accurate and up-to-date are the materials?

    ☐ 3. In what ways do the materials need to be improved?

    ☐ 4. How could the materials be utilized more effectively?

☐ C. What instructional roles or functions are performed by the teacher(s)?

    ☐ 1. How could these roles be performed more effectively?

☐ 2. What important instructional roles are not provided or are performed inadequately? Why?

☐ D. What premises and assumptions about learning and the nature of the learner underly the selection of instructional strategies? How and to what extent are these assumptions warranted?

VII. PROCEDURES AND CRITERIA FOR EVALUATING STUDENTS' ACHIEVE-MENTS

☐ A. What instruments and procedures are employed as a means of collecting evidence of the students' progress and achievement?

☐ B. What criteria are used to assess the adequacy of the students' work and/or achievement? On what basis were these criteria selected?

☐ C. How well do the assessment procedures correspond with the course content and objectives? Which objectives or content areas are not assessed? Why?

☐ D. To what extent do the assessment procedures appear to be fair and objective?

☐ E. What evidence is there that the assessment instruments and procedures yield valid and reliable results?

☐ F. How are the assessment results used? Are the results shared with the students within a reasonable amount of time?

☐ G. How consistently are the assessment criteria applied from instructor to instructor and from term to term?

☐ H. What indications are there that the amount of assessment is excessive, about right or insufficient?

VIII. ORGANIZATION OF THE COURSE

☐ A. How is the course organized in terms of lectures, labs, studios, discussion sections, field trips and other types of scheduled class sessions?

☐ B. How frequently and for how long are the various types of class meetings scheduled? Is the total allocation of time sufficient/insufficient? Why?

☐ C. If there is more than one instructor, what are the duties and responsibilities of each? What problems result from this division of responsibilities?

☐ D. What outside-of-class instruction, tutoring or counseling is provided? By whom? On what basis?

☐ E. How well is the student workload distributed throughout the course?

☐ F. To what extent are the necessary facilities, equipment, and materials readily available and in good working condition when needed?

IX. COURSE OUTCOMES

☐ A. What proportion of the enrollees completed the course with credit during the regular term? How does the completion rate vary from instructor to instructor or from term to term?

☐ B. What proportion of the enrollees withdrew from or discontinued attending the course? Why?

  ☐ 1. To what degree does their discontinuance appear to be related to factors associated with the course?

  ☐ 2. How does the attrition rate vary from instructor to instructor or from term to term?

☐ C. At the end of the course, what evidence is there that students have achieved the stated objectives?

  ☐ 1. For which objectives was the course most/least successful?

  ☐ 2. For what kinds of students was the course most/least successful?

☐ D. What effects does the course appear to have had upon students' interest in the subject-matter and their desire to continue studying and learning about this subject?

☐ E. What other effects did the course have upon the students?

  ☐ 1. How were their values, attitudes, priorities, interests or aspirations changed?

  ☐ 2. How were their study habits or other behavioral patterns modified?

  ☐ 3. How pervasive and/or significant do these effects appear to be?

☐   F.   What evidence is there that students who have completed this course were adequately/inadequately prepared for subsequent courses for which this course is intended to prepare them?

☐   G.   To what extent do students rate their experience in the course as producing a meaningful and worthwhile contribution to their self-development?

    ☐   1.   In what ways were the students satisfied or dissatisfied with the course?

    ☐   2.   What suggestions do they have for improving the course?

☐   H.   What evidence is there, if any, that the experience of teaching the course has a positive or negative effect upon faculty members?

X. INSTITUTIONAL COSTS & BENEFITS

☐   A.   What are the time, space, equipment and facilities requirements of the course?

☐   B.   What are the requirements of the course in terms of faculty and staff?

☐   C.   What other support services are required by the course?

☐   D.   What direct instructional costs are associated with this course?

☐   E.   What benefits derive to the department, the college and the institution for having offered the course?

QUESTIONS TO BE INVESTIGATED IN EVALUATING TWO
INTER-DISCIPLINARY COMMUNICATIONS SKILLS COURSES

1. Course Objectives

   A. What are the formal, stated objectives for each course? In what ways are the objectives similar? How are they different?

   B. How appropriately do the stated objectives of each course match the needs of the target population?

   C. What other unstated purposes, intents or goals do faculty members, administrators, and other interested persons have for each course?

2. Student Population Services

   A. How comparable are the groups in terms of demographic variables such as age, sex, high school rank, SAT scores, academic major and full-time student status?

   B. Why do students choose to enroll in one course instead of the other? Were students turned away from CMS 100X because of a ceiling on enrollment? How many?

3. Types of Learning Encounters & Opportunities Provided

   A. How do the two courses differ in terms of content and organization?

   B. What are the primary modes of instruction used in each course? Approximately what proportion of the students' time (in class plus time spent on assignments) is devoted to listening to lectures, reading, writing, taking tests or small-group discussion?

   C. What are the criteria for determining passing grades in each course?

4. Attendance and Course Completion Rates

   A. To what extent do the courses differ in terms of average daily attendance?

   B. What proportion of the students withdraw from or discontinue each course? To what extent was their discontinuance associated with factors related to the courses?

   C. How do the courses compare in terms of the proportion of students who complete the course with passing grades (full credit)?

5. Observable Student Outcomes

   A. What gains in students' writing skills appear to have occurred in each course?

B. What gains in performance on a test of English grammar and usage appear to have occurred in each course?

C. What gains in students' oral presentation skills appear to have occurred in the trial course?

D. What effects did participation in the courses have on students' writing apprehension and speech apprehension?

E. What effects did participation in the courses have upon students' attitudes towards the practical value and importance of clear and persuasive expression in both oral and written forms?

6. Student Satisfaction

A. To what extent were students' expectations of the courses met? In what ways were their expectations not met?

B. To what extent did students perceive the content and learning activities to be relevant to their needs and interests?

C. How did students rate the quality of the instruction provided?

D. What suggestions and recommendations did students have for improving the course?

7. Impact on Course Instructors

A. What activities do the instructors of the trial course perform as a team? What activities do they perform individually?

B. What effect does participation as an instructor in the trial course appear to have upon faculty members? How does it affect their philosophy of teaching? To what extent do they borrow ideas and methods from the trial course for use in other courses they teach?

C. What proportion of the instructors want to continue teaching the course? What proportion prefer to discontinue their involvement? Why?

8. Support Requirements

A. What are the space, time, physical facilities and equipment requirements of each course?

B. What instructional materials and support services are required by each course? What are the relative costs involved?

C. What are the requirements of each course in terms of full-time equivalent faculty and staff? What dollar outlays per student are required?

D. What policy and/or logistical changes would be necessary to support the continued use of each course?

9. Feasibility of Expansion

A. What is the feasibility of creating additional sections of the course and offering it to a greater number of students each term? What problems would likely be encountered?

Resource E.
Sample Questionnaire
for Use in Planning Evaluations
of Programs and Agencies

GUIDELINES FOR THE ADMINISTRATION, ANALYSIS, AND INTERPRETATION OF
THE <u>PLANNING FOR THE EVALUATION OF PROGRAMS AND AGENCIES</u>
QUESTIONNAIRE (PEPA)

by

Robert M. Diamond
and
Edward F. Kelly

The <u>Planning for the Evaluation of Programs and Agencies</u> questionnaire (PEPA) is designed as part of a systematic process to assist those involved with the administration of academic agencies or departments in selecting the criteria by which the success of that unit will be judged. The recommended procedure for use of PEPA requires that all major groups and individual decision makers who have responsibilities within or for a specific agency or unit actually participate in the evaluation process. The criteria that are established ideally should be agreed to and understood by all.

1. The specific unit or department on which PEPA is to be focused must be clearly understood by all participants. To avoid confusion, it might help to circle in red the specific unit involved in the left hand column of question 5 (i.e., faculty development, media services, etc.) or write the name or department under <u>Other</u>.

2. The questionnaire should, depending on the function and organization of the unit, be completed independently by:

    a. The administrator to whom such a program or unit reports.

[If several units are involved in this discussion and they report to the same administrator, the administrator must complete a separate instrument for each unit.]

    b. The director or chairperson of the unit.

    c. Staff members of the unit.

    d. Advisory, Budget, or other committees actively involved in unit related decisions.

    e. Individuals directly served by the unit.

    f. Funding agency contact – if supported by outside funds.

3. When several groups are involved (committees, staff, etc.), data should be tabulated separately for each group and, if possible, a preliminary consensus on priority criteria should be developed through discussion.

[NOTE: Permission is hereby granted for the duplication and use of the Planning for the Evaluation of Programs and Agencies questionnaire on college and university campus.]

Assuming that time constraints will permit little more than simple tabulation of the frequencies of response to each item and a summary of the number of times particular items were nominated as one of the top five, achieving even a preliminary consensus will be no simple task. Furthermore, PEPA is not composed of 54 independent items. There is some redundancy and none of the items bear very close relationships to each other. Consequently, examination of the results may require that additional items or categories be developed for local use.

We found that users often compose their own "new" items in the comments areas. Since these suggestions are frequently seen as very important by the author, a list of these items should be composed by the facilitator and reported to the user group.

4. A meeting should be held to attempt a final consensus on priority criteria. In attendance should be the administrator to whom the unit reports, the head of the unit, and other appropriate representatives. The facilitator should, using handouts and an overhead projector, first report the summarized data from the various groups and then identify apparent areas of agreement and disagreement. An attempt should be made at this meeting to identify these criteria that will be used and their relative importance.

At this level of use, the identification of "areas of agreement and disagreement" within and between groups on PEPA is based simply on the interocular trauma test; if the result jumps off the summary sheet and hits you between the eyes, it's probably worth discussing with the group.

5. Ultimately, the final criteria that are identified should be published and distributed to all those involved in the decision-making process for later reference. In addition, attempts should be made to determine how the various criteria can be measured and reported and a procedure for implementing the evaluation should be adopted.

It is important to stress that, while the procedure will (a) help people identify the criteria that should be used to determine unit success and (b) provide guidelines for determining the effectiveness of a unit in meeting the goals for which it has been established, PEPA will not answer questions about the comparative worth of different units. For this decision to be made, judgements are necessary on the comparative value of each of the criteria as they related to the overall functioning of the institution. While this instrument may provide some data to assist in this deliberation, PEPA is not designed to answer broad questions regarding institutional-wide budget making when many of the units being evaluated are successfully meeting the charge for which they were established and budget reductions are still deemed necessary.

PLANNING FOR THE EVALUATION OF PROGRAMS AND AGENCIES
by
Robert M. Diamond, Syracuse University
and
Edward F. Kelly, State University of New York at Albany

This questionnaire has been designed to help people who are involved in education focus their thinking about the criteria that should be employed during an evaluation of programs and agencies. In order to focus discussion, comparison, and summary, you are asked to: (1) provide some background information, (2) indicate criteria you believe <u>should</u> be used to evaluate the program or agency in question, and (3) identify which five of these criteria you consider to be most important.

1. Agency or Program being evaluated: _____

2. Your role: Place a check mark in the cell that best suggests what your role is:

	Your Role				
Faculty Development (In-Service Training)					
Course or Curriculum Development					
Media Services					
Library Services					
Library & Media Services					
Computer Services					
Other					
	I am the administrator to whom the program or agency reports	I am the director of the program or agency	I am a staff member of such a program or agency	I am a teacher, a member of a committee, or an administrator who is served by the program or agency	Other

© Center for Instructional Development, Syracuse University, October 1977, revised July 1983.

Resource E: Sample Questionnaire

Listed below are a set of criteria or statements describing characteristics of possible worth. Read each statement carefully and then decide whether or not the characteristic should be used to evaluate the specific agency that you are focusing on in this questionnaire and indicate whether you believe it should be used by checking Yes or No.

		Should be Used	
		Yes	No
1.	Improvement in the design of academic programs	☐	☐
2.	Improvement in faculty ability to design and implement an instructional change	☐	☐
3.	Faculty support of the program or agency	☐	☐
4.	Positive impact on faculty morale	☐	☐
5.	Improved faculty/student relationships	☐	☐
6.	Increased faculty interest and involvement in change	☐	☐
7.	Breadth of faculty involved in effort	☐	☐
8.	Faculty job satisfaction and sense of personal meaningfulness	☐	☐
9.	Impact on tenure and promotion policies and procedures	☐	☐
10.	Effectiveness of in-service training programs conducted	☐	☐
11.	Increasing frequency of faculty conversations about teaching and learning	☐	☐
12.	Improves faculty teaching through a systematic process using development and evaluation	☐	☐
13.	Faculty show a sense of ownership in agency or program	☐	☐
14.	Agency has helped people become better teachers	☐	☐

Feel free to make suggestions on additional criteria or your comments in the space below:

<u>Should be Used</u>

		<u>Yes</u>	<u>No</u>
15.	Positive impact on student learning	❑	❑
16.	Improved retention of learning	❑	❑
17.	Reduction in student attrition rate (drop-outs)	❑	❑
18.	Improved student attitudes toward course, content, and/or program	❑	❑
19.	Increased student support of agency	❑	❑
20.	Extent of student involvement in agency or program's efforts	❑	❑
21.	Increased student enthusiasm for learning	❑	❑
22.	Success of graduates	❑	❑
23.	Involves students directly in the activities of designing or redesigning courses and programs	❑	❑
24.	Improves students' peer relationships	❑	❑
25.	Increases the frequency of informal interaction between students and faculty	❑	❑

Feel free to make suggestions on additional criteria or your comments in the space that follows:

26.	Quality of materials produced	❑	❑
27.	Quality of staff	❑	❑
28.	Accessibility of staff	❑	❑
29.	Extent to which the agency has helped faculty identify new roles	❑	❑
30.	Excellence of the national reputation of agency or program	❑	❑

		Should be used
		<u>Yes</u> <u>No</u>

		Yes	No
31.	Frequency of projects or efforts initiated	❑	❑
32.	Variety of strategies and techniques used	❑	❑
33.	Evaluation of agency or service by external group	❑	❑
34.	Credibility in the off-campus local community	❑	❑
35.	Sensitivity to the political climate of the institution	❑	❑
36.	Key agency staff are recognized as good teachers	❑	❑
37.	Staff are administratively well organized	❑	❑
38.	Staff have a recognized disciplinary background	❑	❑
39.	Agency produces reports that are attractive and highly readable	❑	❑
40.	Agency provides dependable and complete services	❑	❑
41.	Extent to which the reputation of the agency is tied to a specific person	❑	❑
42.	Program or agency is cost efficient	❑	❑

Feel free to make suggestions on additional criteria or your comments in the space that follows:

		Yes	No
43.	Direct costs of running program or agency	❑	❑
44.	Quality of courses or programs developed	❑	❑
45.	Match between programs developed and institutional priorities	❑	❑
46.	Extent of research conducted and reported	❑	❑
47.	Cost benefit of agency or program	❑	❑

		Should be Used	
		Yes	No
48.	Effective as a networking device to identify and link resources and people	☐	☐
49.	Effectiveness of the administrative interventions conducted by agency	☐	☐
50.	Produces an increased concern for professional excellence in teachers and administrators	☐	☐
51.	Produces creative and effective products for professional excellence in teachers and administrators	☐	☐
52.	Sensitivity to the needs and expectations of the State and Federal governments	☐	☐
53.	Secures external funding for institutional projects	☐	☐
54.	Improves faculty/administrator relationships	☐	☐

Feel free to make suggestions on additional criteria or your comments in the space that follows:

Given the criteria rated above, choose the five (5) that you believe are the most critical for determining the worth of the agency or program and write their corresponding number in the five spaces below. You are not required to rank these five criteria

_____   _____   _____   _____   _____

References

Association of American Colleges. *Integrity in the College Curriculum: A Report to the Academic Community.* Washington, D.C.: Association of American Colleges, 1985.

Barry, R. M. "Clarifying Objectives." In O. Milton and Associates, *On College Teaching: A Guide to Contemporary Practices.* San Francisco: Jossey-Bass, 1978.

Bennett, W. J. *To Reclaim a Legacy.* Washington, D.C.: National Endowment for the Humanities, 1984.

Bergquist, W. H., and Armstrong, J. R. *Planning Effectively for Educational Quality: An Outcomes-Based Approach for Colleges Committed to Excellence.* San Francisco: Jossey-Bass, 1986.

Boyer, E. *College, The Undergraduate Experience in America.* New York: Harper & Row, 1987.

Briggs, L. J. *Handbook of Procedures for the Design of Instruction.* Pittsburgh, Pa.: American Institutes for Research, 1970.

Burstyn, J. N., and Santa, C. M. "Complexity as an Impediment to Learning: A Study of Changes in Selected College Textbooks." *Journal of Higher Education,* 1977, *48* (5), 508–518.

Carnegie Foundation for the Advancement of Teaching, The. *College: The Undergraduate Experience in America.* New York: The Carnegie Foundation for the Advancement of Teaching, 1986.

Centra, J., Froh, R. C., Gray, P. J., and Lambert, L. M. *A Guide to*

Evaluating Teaching for Promotion and Tenure. Littleton, Mass.: Copley Publishing Group, 1987.

Cohn, R. P. *To Be or Not to Be? A Method for Evaluating Academic Support Units.* Planning for Higher Education, Profile 30. New York: Educational Facilities Laboratory, 1979.

Commission of Higher Education of the Middle States Association of Colleges and Schools. *Evaluation Team Report on Syracuse University.* Philadelphia: Commission of Higher Education of the Middle States Association of Colleges and Schools, 1977.

Diamond, R. M. *Syracuse University's Center for Instructional Development: Its Role, Organization, and Procedures.* Syracuse, N.Y.: Center for Instructional Development, Syracuse University, 1975.

Diamond, R. M., and Gray, P. J. *National Study of Teaching Assistants.* Syracuse, N.Y.: Center for Instructional Development, Syracuse University, 1987.

Dresser, D. L. "The Relationship Between Personality Needs, College Expectations, Environmental Press and Undergraduate Attrition in a University College of Liberal Arts." Unpublished doctoral dissertation, College of Education, Syracuse University, 1971.

Education Commission of the States. *Transforming the State Role in Undergraduate Education: Time for a Different View.* Denver, Colo.: Education Commission of the States, 1986.

Eickmann, P. E., and Lee, R. T. *Applying an Instructional Development Process to Music Education.* Syracuse, N.Y.: Center for Instructional Development, Syracuse University, 1976.

Future Trends in Broadcast Journalism. Washington, D.C.: Radio-Television News Directors Association, 1984.

Gardiner, J. J. *ASHE Handbook on Teaching and Instructional Resources.* Stillwater: Higher Education Associates, Oklahoma State University, 1987.

Gerlach, V. S., and Ely, D. P. *Teaching and Media: A Systematic Approach.* (2nd ed.) Englewood Cliffs, N.J.: Prentice-Hall, 1980.

Gross, R. P. *Instructional Unit Offers Ideas, Not Hardware, to Spur Change.* Planning for Higher Education, Profile 4. New York: Educational Facilities Laboratory, 1975.

Gustafson, K. L., and Bratton, B. *Instructional Improvement Centers in Higher Education: A Status Survey.* Paper presented at the American Education Research Association, Montreal, Quebec, Canada, April 1983.

Hannun, W. H., and Briggs, L. J. *How Does Instructional Systems Design Differ from Traditional Instruction?* Chapel Hill: University of North Carolina, 1980.

Husen, T. (ed.). *The International Encyclopedia of Education: Research and Studies.* Elmsford, N.Y.: Pergamon Press, 1985.

Kaufman, R., and English, F. W. *Needs Assessment: Concept and Application.* Englewood Cliffs, N.J.: Educational Technology Publications, 1979.

Keller, F. S. "Goodbye Teacher." *Journal of Applied Behavior Analysis,* 1968, *1,* 79–89.

Keller, J. M. *Practitioner's Guide to Concepts and Measures of Motivation.* Syracuse, N.Y.: Syracuse University, 1978.

Kemp, J. E. *Instructional Design: A Plan for Unit and Course Development.* Belmont, Calif.: Fearon, 1977.

Kemp, J. E. *The Instructional Design Process.* New York: Harper & Row, 1985.

Krathwohl, D. R., Bloom, B. S., and Masia, B. B. *Taxonomy of Educational Objectives. The Classification of Education Goals. Handbook II: Affective Domain.* New York: David McKay, 1964.

McKeachie, W. J. *Teaching Tips: A Guidebook for the Beginning College Teacher.* (8th ed.) Lexington, Mass.: Heath, 1986.

Mager, R. F. *Preparing Instructional Objectives.* Belmont, Calif.: Fearon, 1975.

Marchese, T. J. "Third Down, Ten Yards to Go." *American Association of Higher Education Bulletin,* 1987, *40* (4), 8.

Merrill, M. D. "Content Analysis Via Concept Elaboration Theory." *Journal of Instructional Development,* 1977, *1,* 1.

Milton, O., and Associates. *On College Teaching: A Guide to Contemporary Practices.* San Francisco: Jossey-Bass, 1978.

National Institute of Education. *Involvement in Learning: Realizing the Potential of American Higher Education.* Washington, D.C.: National Institute of Education, 1984.

Newman, F. "Selecting the Effects: The Priorities of Retrenchment." *AAHE Bulletin,* 1982, *35* (1), 13.

Pascarella, E. T. *Interaction of Prior Mathematics Preparation, Instructional Method, and Achievement in the Self-Paced and Conventionally Taught Sections of Mathematics 295*. Research Report No. 9. Syracuse, N.Y.: Center for Instructional Development, Syracuse University, 1977.

Perry, W. G. *Forms of Intellectual/Ethical Development in the College Years: A Scheme*. New York: Holt, Rinehart, & Winston, 1970.

Pervin, L. A., and Rubin, D. B. "Student Dissatisfaction with College and the College Dropout: A Transactional Approach." *Journal of Social Psychology*, 1967, 72, 285–295.

Popham, W. J., and Baker, E. L. *Establishing Instructional Goals*. Englewood Cliffs, N.J.: Prentice-Hall, 1970.

Postlethwait, S. N., Novak, J., and Murray, H. T., Jr. *The Audio-Tutorial Approach to Learning*. (3rd ed.) Minneapolis: Burgess, 1972.

Powers, D. E., and Enright, M. K. "Analytical Reasoning Skills in Graduate Study: Perceptions of Faculty in Six Fields." *Journal of Higher Education*, 1987, *58* (6), 658–682.

Rubin, S. "Professors, Students, and the Syllabus." *The Chronicle of Higher Education*, 1985, *30* (23), 56.

Russell, J. D., and Johanningsmeir, K. A. *Improving Competence Through Modular Instruction*. Dubuque, Iowa: Kendall/Hunt, 1981.

Sachs, S. G. *Supporting Real Innovation in the 80's — Characteristics of ID Units That Will Make It Happen*. (Occasional paper.) Washington, D.C.: Division of Instructional Development, Association for Educational Communication and Technology, 1984.

State of New Jersey College Outcomes Evaluation Program Advisory Committee. *Report to the New Jersey Board of Higher Education from the Advisory Committee to the College Outcomes Evaluation Program*. Trenton: Board of Higher Education, State of New Jersey, 1987.

Stern, G. *People in Context*. New York: Wiley, 1970.

van Enckevort, G., Harry, K., Morin, P., and Schutze, H. G. (eds.). *Distance Higher Education and the Adult Learner*. Heerlen, The Netherlands: Open University, 1986.

Wittich, W., and Schuller, C. *Instructional Technology: Its Nature and Use*. (6th ed.) New York: Harper & Row, 1979.

Index

A

Academic credit, in chemistry course for high-risk students, 79–80
Academic improvement. *See* Model for academic improvement
Administrators: and academic improvement, 2, 3; on design team, 41, 44; and operational design, 104; ownership by, 17; and project selection, 33–34; and support unit, 104, 192, 208, 211–212, 213
Advanced Placement Examination Program, 201
Agency. *See* Support unit
Alumni survey: in education, 93, 96–97; sample, 225–232
Alverno College, evaluation approach at, 114
American Association for Higher Education, and journals, 63, 64
Arizona State University, computers for instruction at, 114
Armstrong, J. L., 126–127
Art course, objectives in, 132, 133
Art history course: design of, 147–148; fiscal support for, 146–147; goals of, 146; media selection for, 145–149; results of designing, 148–149
Assessment: of needs, 21, 31; and objectives, 124–125. *See also* Evaluation
Association for the Study of Higher Education (ASHE), and pedagogy, 64
Atkinson, F. D., 154
Attitudes, of students, 49–50, 51–52, 53
Audiotutorial approach, as managerial system, 140–141, 147, 198

B

Baker, E. L., 5
Barry, R. M., 127
Basic planning units: data for, 46–65; design team for, 40–45
Benjamin, A., 19
Bergquist, W. H., 126–127
Bertcher, H. J., 19
Biology courses: advanced placement in, 201; laboratory use patterns in, 156

269

R

S